Mathematics Teaching
REIMAGINED

Seven Competencies to
Foster Robust Student Learning
and Engagement

NATHAN D. LANG-RAAD

Copyright © 2025 by Solution Tree Press

Materials appearing here are copyrighted. With one exception, all rights are reserved. Readers may reproduce only those pages marked "Reproducible." Otherwise, no part of this book may be reproduced or transmitted in any form or by any means (electronic, photocopying, recording, or otherwise) without prior written permission of the publisher. This book, in whole or in part, may not be included in a large language model, used to train AI, or uploaded into any AI system.

555 North Morton Street
Bloomington, IN 47404
800.733.6786 (toll free) / 812.336.7700
FAX: 812.336.7790

email: info@SolutionTree.com
SolutionTree.com

Visit **go.SolutionTree.com/mathematics** to download the free reproducibles in this book.

Printed in the United States of America

Library of Congress Cataloging-in-Publication Data

Names: Lang-Raad, Nathan D., 1982- author
Title: Mathematics teaching reimagined : seven competencies to foster robust student learning and engagement / Nathan D. Lang-Raad.
Description: Bloomington, IN : Solution Tree Press, [2025] | Includes bibliographical references and index.
Identifiers: LCCN 2024050490 (print) | LCCN 2024050491 (ebook) | ISBN 9798893740073 paperback | ISBN 9798893740080 ebook
Subjects: LCSH: Mathematics--Study and teaching (Elementary) | Mathematics--Study and teaching (Secondary)
Classification: LCC QA135.6 .L364 2025 (print) | LCC QA135.6 (ebook) | DDC 510.71/2--dc23/eng/20250311
LC record available at https://lccn.loc.gov/2024050490
LC ebook record available at https://lccn.loc.gov/2024050491

Solution Tree
Jeffrey C. Jones, CEO
Edmund M. Ackerman, President

Solution Tree Press
President and Publisher: Douglas M. Rife
Associate Publishers: Todd Brakke and Kendra Slayton
Editorial Director: Laurel Hecker
Art Director: Rian Anderson
Copy Chief: Jessi Finn
Senior Production Editor: Miranda Addonizio
Proofreader: Sarah Ludwig
Text and Cover Designer: Abigail Bowen
Acquisitions Editors: Carol Collins and Hilary Goff
Content Development Specialist: Amy Rubenstein
Associate Editors: Sarah Ludwig and Elijah Oates
Editorial Assistant: Madison Chartier

ACKNOWLEDGMENTS

Writing this book has been a transformative journey, one made possible through the support, guidance, and encouragement of very special individuals. First and foremost, I want to express my deepest gratitude to my husband, Herbie Raad, whose unwavering support, insightful feedback, and constant encouragement have been instrumental in bringing this work to fruition. Your belief in me and your understanding during the long hours of writing and research have meant more than words can express.

I am profoundly grateful to Miranda Addonizio, whose exceptional developmental editing helped shape and refine this manuscript. Your thoughtful guidance and keen editorial eye elevated the work in countless ways, ensuring that complex ideas were presented with clarity and purpose. Todd Brakke, thank you for your steadfast support and vision throughout this project. Your commitment to excellence in educational publishing has been inspiring.

A special note of appreciation goes to Sarah Payne-Mills, who has been an extraordinary thought partner throughout this journey. Your ability to challenge my thinking while providing unwavering support has been invaluable. Your enthusiasm for this work and your belief in its potential impact on mathematics education have been constant sources of motivation.

I would also like to thank the dedicated educators who reviewed this manuscript and provided valuable feedback. Your insights from the field helped ensure that this work remained grounded in classroom realities while pushing the boundaries of what's possible in mathematics education.

Finally, to the countless teachers and students who have shaped my understanding of mathematics instruction over the years: Your experiences, challenges, and successes have been invaluable. Your dedication to teaching and learning mathematics continues to inspire me to work toward better educational outcomes for all students.

Solution Tree Press would like to thank the following reviewers:

Taylor Bronowicz
Sixth-Grade Mathematics Teacher
Albertville Intermediate School
Albertville, Alabama

Eunice Salazar-Banks
Education Specialist for School
    Improvement
Corpus Christi, Texas

Paula Mathews
STEM Instructional Coach
Dripping Springs ISD
Dripping Springs, Texas

Rachel Swearengin
Fifth-Grade Teacher
Manchester Park Elementary
Lenexa, Kansas

Janet Nuzzie
District Intervention Specialist,
    K–12 Mathematics
Pasadena ISD
Pasadena, Texas

Visit **go.SolutionTree.com/mathematics** to download
the free reproducibles in this book.

TABLE OF CONTENTS

About the Author ix

Introduction 1

The Need for a New Framework 4

About the Book 7

CHAPTER **ONE**

Myths and Misconceptions in Mathematics Education 9

How the CMC Framework Helps Educators
Address Common Misunderstandings 11

The Role of Educators in Shaping Mathematical Mindsets . . . 23

Conclusion 24

CHAPTER **TWO**

Conceptual and Procedural Integration 25

The Essence of Conceptual and Procedural Integration 25

Strategies to Enhance Conceptual
and Procedural Integration 38

Conclusion 45

CHAPTER **THREE**

Problem Solving and Modeling 47

The Essence of Problem Solving and Modeling 49

Strategies to Enhance Problem Solving and Modeling 60

Conclusion 69

CHAPTER **FOUR**

Logical Reasoning and Proof 71

The Essence of Logical Reasoning and Proof 72

Strategies to Enhance Logical Reasoning and Proof 78

Conclusion 92

CHAPTER **FIVE**

Communication and Representation 95

The Essence of Communication and Representation 96

Strategies to Enhance Communication
and Representation 111

Conclusion 120

CHAPTER **SIX**

Strategic Use of Tools and Precision 121

The Essence of Strategic Use of Tools and Precision 123

Strategies to Enhance Strategic Use
of Tools and Precision 134

Conclusion 141

CHAPTER **SEVEN**

Structural Insight and Regularity 143

The Essence of Structural Insight and Regularity 143

Strategies to Enhance Structural Insight and Regularity . . . 148

Conclusion 158

CHAPTER **EIGHT**

Productive Disposition and Engagement 161

The Essence of Productive Disposition and Engagement 162

Strategies to Enhance Productive
Disposition and Engagement 169

Conclusion 185

CHAPTER **NINE**

The CMC Framework in Your Classroom 187

Curriculum 188

Planning 196

Instruction 199

Assessment 206

Professional Learning 212

Conclusion 218

Epilogue... 219

References and Resources 221

Index 227

ABOUT THE AUTHOR

Nathan D. Lang-Raad, EdD, is an educator, speaker, and author. He is the founder and CEO of Raad Education, where he continues to lead innovations in educational practice and theory.

Nathan's rich career history spans roles as a teacher, elementary and high school administrator, and university adjunct professor. Notably, he has served as the director of elementary curriculum and instruction for Metropolitan Nashville Public Schools in Tennessee and as an education supervisor at NASA's Johnson Space Center. His previous roles include chief education officer at WeVideo and vice president, national product line at Savvas Learning.

An accomplished author, Nathan has contributed significantly to education literature, writing extensively about instructional coaching, innovative teaching methods, and the integration of technology in classrooms. His publications include *Everyday Instructional Coaching: Seven Daily Drivers to Support Teacher Effectiveness*; *The New Art and Science of Teaching Mathematics* (coauthored with Robert J. Marzano); *WeVideo Every Day: 40 Strategies to Deepen Learning in Any Class*; *Mathematics Unit Planning in a PLC at Work, Grades PreK–2* (coauthored with Sarah Schuhl, Timothy D. Kanold, Jennifer Deinhart, Matthew R. Larson, and Nanci N. Smith); *The Teachers of Oz: Leading With Wisdom, Heart, Courage, and Spirit* (coauthored with Herbie Raad); *The Boundless Classroom: Designing Purposeful Instruction for Any Learning Environment* (coauthored with James

Vince Witty); *Instructional Coaching Connection: Building Relationships to Better Support Teachers*; *Never Stop Asking: Teaching Students to Be Better Critical Thinkers*; *Renaissance Thinking in the Classroom: Interdisciplinary Learning, Real-World Problems, Intellectually Curious Students*; and *The AI Assist: Strategies for Integrating AI Into the Very Human Act of Teaching*.

Nathan earned a bachelor's degree in general science–chemistry from Harding University, a master's degree in administration and supervision from the University of Houston–Victoria, and a doctorate in learning organizations and strategic change from Lipscomb University.

Nathan lives with his husband, Herbie Raad, in scenic Maine, where he continues his pursuit of empowering educators and transforming learning landscapes.

To learn more about Nathan's pioneering work, follow @drlangraad on X.

TO BOOK NATHAN D. LANG-RAAD FOR PROFESSIONAL DEVELOPMENT, CONTACT PD@SOLUTIONTREE.COM.

INTRODUCTION

We are living in an era in which mathematical thinking is no longer optional—it's essential for participating fully in our technology-driven, data-rich world. Mathematical literacy has become as fundamental as reading for informed citizenship. While mathematics has always been central to education, emerging challenges demand a transformation in how we teach it.

Mathematics education stands at a critical juncture. Although technological advances and the evolving workforce require increasingly sophisticated mathematical thinking, many students continue to struggle with fundamental concepts and harbor anxiety about mathematics. Research consistently shows that despite decades of refinement, mathematics education has not adequately prepared students for the analytical and problem-solving challenges they face in higher education and careers. The need for change is clear and urgent. Traditional approaches have often emphasized isolated skill development and procedural fluency, leading many students to view mathematics as a disconnected series of rules to memorize rather than a coherent and meaningful discipline. This limited scope not only creates gaps in understanding but can foster negative relationships with mathematics that persist throughout students' academic lives and beyond.

This book offers a transformative path forward—one that reimagines the very essence of mathematics education. It moves beyond compartmentalized learning to an integrated approach that illuminates the interconnected nature of mathematical concepts and their practical applications. By highlighting the utility and universality of mathematics while empowering both teachers and students, this new vision creates opportunities for deeper understanding and genuine engagement with mathematical thinking.

At the heart of this journey is a challenge: to transform your approach to teaching mathematics from a routine exercise to a rich, engaging, and deeply relevant experience for your students. The comprehensive mathematical competencies (CMC) framework responds to the evolving demands of mathematics instruction through seven essential competencies: (1) conceptual and procedural integration, (2) problem solving and modeling, (3) logical reasoning and proof, (4) communication and representation, (5) strategic use of tools and precision, (6) structural insight and regularity, and (7) productive disposition and engagement. Together, these competencies foster the comprehensive mathematical proficiency K–12 educators need to unlock a thorough understanding of mathematics for all students, preparing them for the complexities of life. Figure I.1 illustrates the CMC framework.

Each of the seven competencies that compose the CMC framework receives its own chapter in this book, carefully crafted to provide educators and students with a clear path to mathematical proficiency. The upcoming chapters are meticulously designed to address and build on each foundational competency, paving the way for holistic mathematical proficiency development.

Since 2020, the landscape of education has undergone unprecedented changes. The global COVID-19 pandemic forced a rapid shift to remote and hybrid learning environments, revealing both the possibilities and the limitations of traditional mathematics instruction. This period of disruption exacerbated an already concerning trend: significant gaps in students' foundational mathematical knowledge. National assessment data show declining proficiency in basic arithmetic operations, number sense, and algebraic thinking—skills that form the bedrock of mathematics learning (Nation's Report Card, n.d.a, n.d.b). These gaps, which often begin in elementary grades, compound over time, making it increasingly difficult for students to grasp complex concepts and develop mathematical confidence.

Introduction

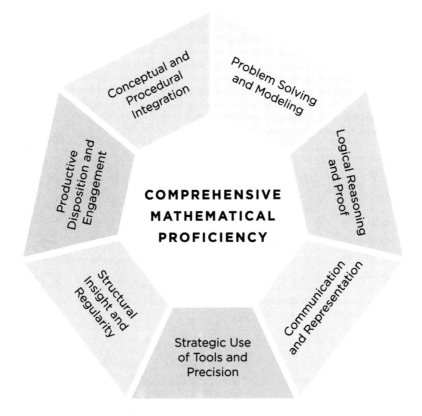

Figure I.1: CMC framework.

This crisis in foundational skills has heightened the urgency to reimagine mathematics education. Students now require not just computational skills but the ability to analyze complex problems, recognize patterns, and adapt mathematical thinking to novel situations. The challenges are clear: persistent achievement gaps, declining student engagement, gaps in foundational skills that impede progress, and a growing disconnect between classroom mathematics and real-world applications. In this context, it has become imperative to develop a framework that not only addresses these current challenges but also leverages students' potential to engage deeply with mathematics. The CMC framework introduced in this book is designed to achieve exactly that. In the following pages, we'll further explore the necessity of a new framework for mathematics education, and a book overview will highlight the nature of each critical component and what you can expect to find in the chapters to come.

The Need for a New Framework

Despite advances in educational research and technology, studies reveal that mathematics instruction in many schools worldwide continues to prioritize procedural fluency and memorization over deeper conceptual understanding. Data from the National Assessment of Educational Progress demonstrate a persistent gap between current instructional practices and evidence-based approaches to mathematics education (Nation's Report Card, n.d.a). This gap between research-based best practices and actual classroom instruction is particularly concerning given mounting evidence from cognitive science of how students best learn mathematics. The National Mathematics Advisory Panel (2008) and subsequent studies have consistently shown that traditional instruction emphasizing quick recall and procedural knowledge without conceptual understanding results in fragmented mathematics learning that proves insufficient for the complex problem-solving demands of an increasingly technologically advanced and data-driven world (Hurrell, 2021; Rittle-Johnson & Schneider, 2015).

This disconnect between traditional instructional models and the needs of 21st century learners isn't limited to any one region; a pattern has emerged in international studies from Europe, Asia, and the Americas, suggesting a global need for pedagogical transformation (Murphy & Ingram, 2023).

Recognizing this gap, the CMC framework encompasses a wider array of skills that go beyond the basics to include critical thinking, problem solving, and application in real-world scenarios. This framework draws on the robust pedagogical foundations provided by the National Council of Teachers of Mathematics' (2000) processes, which advocate for a balanced approach that includes problem solving, reasoning, communication, and connections in mathematics. It also integrates the dynamic and practical orientations of the Common Core

State Standards for mathematics, which emphasize reasoning abstractly and quantitatively, constructing viable arguments, and modeling with mathematics (National Governors Association Center for Best Practices [NGA] & Council of Chief State School Officers [CCSSO], 2010).

Moreover, the CMC framework incorporates insights outlined in the National Research Council's (2001) *Adding It Up*, which argues for a comprehensive view of mathematics learning that includes five research-based strands: (1) conceptual understanding, (2) procedural fluency, (3) strategic competence, (4) adaptive reasoning, and (5) a productive disposition toward mathematics. These foundational strands are intentionally woven throughout the seven comprehensive mathematical competencies, with some strands informing multiple competencies to create a more detailed and actionable framework for today's classroom needs.

The CMC framework expands on these strands in the following ways.

- It unifies conceptual understanding and procedural fluency in a single competency to emphasize their interdependence.
- It elaborates on strategic competence through both the problem-solving and modeling competency and the strategic use of tools and precision competency.
- It develops adaptive reasoning through the logical reasoning and proof competency and the structural insight and regularity competency.
- Communication and representation emerge as their own single competency, recognizing the crucial role of mathematical discourse and multiple representations in modern mathematics education.
- Productive disposition remains central, paired with engagement to emphasize the active nature of mathematics learning.

This alignment shows how the CMC framework builds on established research while responding to contemporary instructional needs and integrating insights from decades of mathematics education research.

The CMC framework also aligns with the emerging science of mathematics movement, which uses objective evidence about how students learn mathematics to inform educational practices and policies. For example, Sarah R. Powell and her colleagues (2020) synthesize evidence from elementary mathematics interventions highlighting the importance of integrating conceptual and procedural knowledge for deeper learning. Similarly, Jennifer E. Kong, Christy Yan, Allison Serceki, and H. Lee Swanson (2021) demonstrate through meta-analysis the effectiveness of structured problem-solving approaches that emphasize both strategic thinking and clear mathematical communication. Work by Lynn S. Fuchs, Rebecca Newman-Gonchar, and their colleagues (2021) further supports this integrated approach, showing how systematic instruction that combines multiple competencies leads to stronger mathematical understanding, particularly for struggling learners. This alignment with established theories and with current research ensures the framework reflects our evolving understanding of how students best learn and apply mathematical concepts in today's educational context.

By synthesizing these elements, the CMC framework offers a cohesive and holistic approach that not only covers the essential mathematical procedures but also encourages students to see mathematics as a connected, useful, and enriching discipline. This approach aims to equip students with the necessary skills to navigate and succeed in an increasingly complex society where mathematics is ubiquitously applied to solve problems across various domains—from science and technology to business and social issues.

The need for such a framework is critical. As educators, we must ensure that our students are capable of computing numbers and recalling formulas as well as proficient in making informed decisions and solving practical problems by applying their mathematical understanding. This shift from a narrow focus to a comprehensive instructional strategy is what the CMC framework aims to achieve to ensure that all students are prepared for the challenges and opportunities of the future.

About the Book

This book comprises nine chapters that lay out the CMC framework's competencies and associated competency-based classroom strategies. Each chapter is a stepping stone toward redefining and enriching the way we teach and perceive mathematics. The exploration begins in chapter 1, which addresses common misconceptions about mathematics learning and teaching and establishes the foundations for developing a genuine appreciation of the subject. By examining and debunking these persistent myths, the chapter sets the stage for the transformative approach presented in subsequent chapters and helps readers understand why traditional perspectives on mathematics education need to evolve.

In chapter 2, we dig into the first framework competency: conceptual and procedural integration. This chapter explores the synergy between understanding mathematical concepts and executing procedures, enhancing flexibility and accuracy in problem solving. Chapter 3 covers the competency of problem solving and modeling, which focuses on learning to understand complex problems and solve them through a variety of strategies and models, reflecting their real-world applications. Logical reasoning and proof, the skill set of chapter 4, emphasizes the development of logical thinking and the ability to justify conclusions through mathematical proof, which fosters a deep understanding of mathematical structures. Chapter 5 discusses the importance of clear communication and diverse representations in mathematics, enabling students to effectively express and understand mathematical ideas. In chapter 6, we explore the significance of the strategic use of tools and precision, a competency that highlights the judicious use of mathematical tools and the importance of precision in mathematical thought and expression. Chapter 7 delves into structural insight and regularity, the ability to recognize and use patterns and structures to simplify and solve complex mathematical problems. Closing out the competency chapters, chapter 8 advocates for productive disposition and engagement—cultivating a positive attitude toward mathematics and emphasizing its utility, beauty, and intrinsic value.

Note that each competency within the CMC framework is designed to contribute to students' comprehensive mathematical proficiency. While the preceding chapters focus on individual competencies, it is important to recognize that these competencies are interrelated and collectively enhance overall mathematical proficiency. The integrated nature of the framework ensures that skills developed in one area support and enrich learning in others, providing a cohesive approach to mathematics education.

The final chapter of this book brings together the insights from all the CMC framework's competencies. It emphasizes the importance of a unified approach to mathematics education that seamlessly integrates all seven competencies into teaching practices. Chapter 9 provides practical steps for implementing the CMC framework and cultivating among your students a profound and enduring enthusiasm for mathematics. It is a call to action for educators to embrace these strategies so that they enhance both academic achievement and the development of a lifelong passion for mathematical exploration.

Mathematics Teaching Reimagined aims to challenge you to embrace these competencies and transform the mathematical journey for your students. As we venture into this new era of teaching, let us commit to reimagining what mathematics education can and should be so that we prepare our students not just for tests but for life.

CHAPTER 1

Myths and Misconceptions in Mathematics Education

Before I delve into the common myths and misconceptions in mathematics education, it's crucial that we recognize how these beliefs can impede the successful implementation of any new teaching framework. Deeply held misconceptions about how students learn and engage with mathematics often act as invisible barriers to change, influencing everything from instructional choices to student engagement. By directly confronting these misconceptions, we clear the path for the CMC framework's implementation. Understanding and addressing these myths is not just a preliminary step—it is essential groundwork that allows educators to approach the framework's seven competencies with an open mind and clear perspective. When we shed light on these misconceptions, we can better understand why traditional approaches fall short and why a comprehensive framework that simultaneously develops multiple competencies is necessary for meaningful mathematics education.

We must challenge widespread beliefs that other educators, students, and families may hold, such as the notion that mathematics is merely a collection of formulas to memorize and apply. This view, while emphasizing the importance of procedural fluency and automaticity, often overshadows the broader spectrum of mathematical competencies required for deep understanding. Reflect with me on the numerous instances in which students, perhaps overwhelmed by seemingly complex problems, concede to the notion that they are "not good at math." This chapter aims to dismantle such myths by offering alternative approaches that help educators understand and address these limiting beliefs about mathematics learning.

Consider the traditional portrayal of mathematics in educational systems, often dominated by rote memorization and the mechanical application of procedures. This method, which is deeply rooted in past educational practices, fails to capitalize on the inherently logical and creative nature of mathematics. While procedural fluency is crucial and allows for the efficient execution of calculations, it is but one strand that must be interwoven with other foundational strands—such as conceptual understanding—and key CMC elements like problem solving, communication, and strategic thinking. These strands and elements work together to enrich students' mathematical proficiency.

It is imperative, therefore, to redefine success in mathematics not just as the ability to swiftly recall and apply algorithms but as the capacity to understand the conceptual foundations of mathematical ideas, integrate these skills seamlessly, and apply them creatively. In this reimagined framework, success is evident in a student's ability to relate mathematical concepts to real-world problems, think critically about numerical information, and approach mathematical challenges with confidence and resilience.

Through this chapter, I explore the transformation necessary in mathematics education. I explain how the CMC framework challenges entrenched and outdated ideas, such as the notion of inherent ability, the focus on memorization, the importance of speed, and the view that struggle is something to be avoided. I advocate instead for fostering a deep conceptual understanding of and appreciation for the discipline. I also illuminate the role of educators in shaping students' mathematical mindsets. By acknowledging the essential role of procedural fluency while also promoting other critical mathematical strands and elements, we can reveal the true nature of mathematics as a dynamic, accessible, and profoundly logical field, opening all students up to a world of opportunity and insight.

How the CMC Framework Helps Educators Address Common Misunderstandings

Incorporating the CMC framework into mathematics education provides educators with systematic ways to address and overcome common misconceptions about mathematics learning. By challenging these myths through evidence-based practices, educators can transform their classrooms into dynamic spaces where inquiry and discovery flourish. The framework's comprehensive approach ensures that all students have opportunities to succeed by developing multiple competencies simultaneously, leading to deeper understanding and greater appreciation of mathematics.

The framework specifically helps educators do the following.

- Recognize how misconceptions influence teaching practices and student engagement.
- Replace limiting beliefs with evidence-based approaches to mathematics instruction.
- Create learning environments that balance skill development with conceptual understanding.
- Foster student confidence through structured, progressive skill building.
- Develop mathematical thinking that goes beyond procedural knowledge.

The following sections dig into each misconception.

Refuting the Notion of Inherent Ability

The belief in inherent mathematical ability remains a deeply ingrained myth within 21st century education, despite mounting evidence against it. Research by Yue Li and Timothy C. Bates (2020) challenges the notion of fixed mathematical ability, while large-scale studies like that of David S. Yeager and colleagues (2019) demonstrate how beliefs about mathematical capacity significantly impact student achievement across diverse educational settings. Even more concerning, Daeun Park, Elizabeth A. Gunderson, Eli Tsukayama, Susan C. Levine, and Sian L. Beilock (2016) find that well-intentioned teachers who explicitly reject the idea of fixed mathematical ability often unconsciously perpetuate inequality through the following instructional practices.

- Primarily calling on students who quickly grasp concepts
- Providing different levels of questioning based on perceived ability
- Offering certain students more wait time than others
- Making grouping decisions that limit advancement opportunities
- Providing differential feedback that implies some students are naturally "math people"
- Reducing assignment rigor based on assumptions about students' capability

While these practices often stem from a desire to support struggling students, they can inadvertently reinforce the very barriers they aim to break down.

This notion of inherent ability posits that students are predestined to either excel at or struggle with mathematics. Such binary thinking not only sets up false and limiting expectations but also misrepresents the true nature of learning and achieving in mathematics. According to psychologist Carol S. Dweck (2016), it fosters a *fixed mindset*, in which ability is seen as static and unchangeable, rather than a *growth mindset*, which is based on the understanding that abilities can be developed through dedication, effective teaching, and continuous effort.

This myth undermines educational equity and accessibility, suggesting effort and quality instruction are secondary to innate ability. Such a belief creates a doubly destructive effect: It discourages students from persisting through challenges while simultaneously causing teachers to question the impact of their instructional efforts. When teachers operate under this misconception, even unconsciously, they may invest less energy in developing innovative teaching strategies or providing challenging opportunities to students they perceive as less mathematically inclined. Meanwhile, students internalize these lowered expectations, leading to reduced effort and engagement. The result is a self-fulfilling cycle that disempowers both teachers and students and creates classroom environments where neither group fully realizes their potential for growth and achievement.

The CMC framework directly counters this disempowerment by acknowledging and maximizing teachers' and students' agency. It recognizes that teacher expertise in implementing effective instructional strategies, combined with student effort and engagement, creates powerful opportunities for mathematical growth. By providing clear competency pathways and structured support for both teaching and learning, the framework empowers all classroom learners to contribute meaningfully to the learning process.

To counter the myth of inherent mathematical ability, educators must focus on implementing evidence-based instructional practices that develop mathematical proficiency in all students. Rather than attributing student success or struggle to innate capacity, research shows that achievement stems from the quality and systematic nature of instruction that students receive. Teachers who shift their focus from perceived ability to proven instructional methods can create learning environments where all students develop mathematical competence. The following research-based approaches provide concrete ways to support mathematical achievement while moving beyond the limiting belief in inherent ability.

Powell and colleagues (2020) and Elizabeth A. Stevens, Melissa A. Rodgers, and Sarah R. Powell (2018) offer compelling evidence that students can achieve significant mathematical proficiency when they receive explicit, systematic instruction and appropriate educational support. Jean Stockard, Timothy W. Wood, Cristy Coughlin, and Caitlin Rasplica Khoury's (2018) comprehensive meta-analysis, spanning fifty years of research, demonstrates that mathematical achievement is largely influenced by the quality and type of instruction that teachers employ, particularly the use of clear, systematic teaching approaches, rather than by any predetermined capacity. These findings emphasize that effective mathematics instruction—not inherent ability—is the key factor in student success. This is further supported by Gena Nelson and Kristen L. McMaster's (2019) meta-analysis showing that early intervention with explicit instruction can significantly improve mathematical outcomes for all students.

Research-based approaches for addressing mathematical achievement include the following.

- **Implementing effective skill-building instruction:** Research demonstrates that the most significant improvements in mathematical achievement come from systematic, explicit instruction focused on building mathematical skills (Fuchs, Newman-Gonchar, et al., 2021). While maintaining a positive classroom environment is important, the primary focus should be on delivering high-quality mathematics instruction and interventions.

- **Supporting productive learning behaviors:** Rather than focusing solely on mindset, teachers should implement specific practices that encourage effective learning behaviors. Robin S. Codding, Robert J. Volpe, and Brian C. Poncy (2017) recommend providing clear learning goals, specific feedback on mathematical work, and opportunities for students to monitor their own progress through data-based decision making.

- **Integrating conceptual and procedural learning:**
  Studies emphasize that effective mathematics instruction must systematically develop both procedural fluency and conceptual understanding (Powell et al., 2020). This integrated approach lets students build strong foundational skills while developing deeper mathematical understanding.

Ultimately, dispelling the myth of inherent ability in mathematics is crucial for creating an inclusive and effective educational experience. It allows for a just and equitable approach to teaching that recognizes and nurtures every student's potential to learn and excel in mathematics. It demands implementing systematic, evidence-based instruction that develops mathematical proficiency for all students. When educators focus on delivering high-quality, explicit instruction and monitoring student progress through data-based decision making, they create learning environments where all students can succeed. This approach moves beyond philosophical statements about student potential to concrete instructional practices that have been proven to develop mathematical competence. By consistently and systematically implementing these research-validated practices, we can ensure all students develop the mathematical skills necessary for academic success and lifelong learning.

Characterizing Mathematics as More Than Memorization

Research shows that many educators continue to emphasize procedural memorization over conceptual understanding, despite evidence that both should be developed simultaneously. Bethany Rittle-Johnson and Michael Schneider (2015) document how this misconception manifests through instructional practices that prioritize memorizing formulas and procedures before building conceptual foundations. Jon R. Star (2005) notes that this approach reflects a fundamental misunderstanding of procedural knowledge itself, incorrectly positioning it as opposite to deep understanding rather than complementary to it. Such practices persist even in modern classrooms, where teachers might require students to memorize algorithms without understanding their underlying principles or drill procedures before establishing conceptual foundations.

This narrow view does a significant disservice to the discipline, as it fails to recognize that conceptual knowledge and procedural knowledge develop in tandem, each supporting the other's growth (Schneider & Stern, 2010). While procedural fluency is essential, research demonstrates that it should be developed alongside conceptual understanding rather than in isolation. This integrated approach better reflects mathematics' inherent creativity and its fundamental role in problem solving and logical reasoning.

True mathematical proficiency involves much more than memorization. It requires an ability to apply mathematical concepts in varied and novel situations. Effective mathematics education encourages students to grapple with problems, explore multiple solutions, and make connections between different mathematical ideas. It fosters an environment where reasoning and creativity are at the forefront, enabling students to use mathematics as a powerful tool for problem solving and innovation. For example, when teaching multidigit multiplication, rather than simply having students memorize the standard algorithm, an effective lesson might proceed as follows: Students first use base-ten blocks to model the multiplication of two-digit numbers, which helps them understand why the procedure works. They then explore and compare different methods for solving the same problem—such as the standard algorithm, partial products, and the area model—while explicitly discussing how these approaches connect to the concrete models they created. Through this systematic progression, students develop both procedural fluency with multiplication and a deeper conceptual understanding of place value and the distributive property. This type of instruction, supported by research from Rittle-Johnson (2017), demonstrates how procedural and conceptual knowledge can develop together, leading to more robust mathematical understanding.

Real understanding emerges from systematic instruction that integrates conceptual understanding with procedural practice. Michael

Schneider, Bethany Rittle-Johnson, and Jon R. Star (2011) demonstrate that when students engage in structured learning experiences that connect procedures with concepts, they develop more flexible mathematical knowledge that transfers to new contexts. This finding is reinforced by Rittle-Johnson's (2017) research showing that mathematical understanding develops through carefully sequenced instruction that allows students to build and test their knowledge systematically. As Powell and colleagues (2020) emphasize in their synthesis of mathematics interventions, effective instruction must provide explicit connections between concepts and procedures while offering opportunities for guided practice and application. This evidence-based approach cultivates the mathematical proficiency necessary for academic success and real-world problem solving.

Minimizing Misunderstandings About Speed and Fluency

Research demonstrates that both fluency-building activities and conceptual understanding are essential for mathematical proficiency (Codding et al., 2017). While some educators have historically viewed timed practice as potentially harmful, evidence shows that timed activities are necessary components of effective mathematics instruction, particularly for building the automaticity that enables students to engage with complex mathematical thinking (VanDerHeyden & Codding, 2020).

The CMC framework recognizes this research by integrating fluency-building activities with conceptual development. Rather than avoiding timed practice, the framework advocates for its strategic use within a comprehensive instructional approach. When students achieve automaticity in basic operations through appropriate fluency practice, they can dedicate more cognitive resources to understanding and solving complex problems. This integration is supported by research showing that fluency is an essential dimension of mathematical mastery associated with robust understanding and flexible problem solving (Fuchs, Newman-Gonchar, et al., 2021).

Key principles for implementing this balanced approach include the following.

- Using timed activities specifically for building fluency after students have established accuracy and conceptual understanding
- Providing a systematic progression from accuracy to fluency
- Integrating fluency practice with meaningful problem-solving activities
- Using data from timed assessments to inform instructional decisions
- Ensuring tasks are appropriately matched to students' current skill levels

While speed indicates familiarity with mathematical facts, it does not necessarily reflect a deep understanding of concepts or the capacity to apply mathematical thinking to solve complex problems. The CMC framework prioritizes a learning environment where deep, thoughtful problem solving is held in higher regard than the rapid recall of mnemonic devices and tricks for memorizing specific mathematical procedures. This approach encourages reflective engagement with mathematical concepts, fostering genuine understanding that goes beyond superficial knowledge.

In the CMC framework, tasks are deliberately designed to allow students the time and space to delve deeply into mathematical concepts and explore and reflect on their understanding. For example, when learning the concept of area in geometry, students could first engage in hands-on activities using manipulatives such as square tiles to cover a rectangular surface. They could explore the relationship between the dimensions of the rectangle and the number of tiles needed to cover the area, making observations about how length and width are multiplied. Afterward, students could be guided to derive the formula for the area of a rectangle ($A = l \times w$) from this exploration. This activity not only helps students understand the concept of area more deeply but also connects the abstract formula to a concrete experience. This learning method encourages students to question, hypothesize, and test their ideas, fostering a more profound engagement with mathematics. It allows them to explore the why and how of mathematics, not just the what. By doing so, students develop a rich appreciation for and a robust understanding of mathematical principles.

It is crucial to distinguish between mere speed and automaticity in the context of learning mathematics. *Automaticity* refers to the ability to perform basic mathematical operations swiftly and without conscious effort. This capability is fundamental, as it helps reduce cognitive load, freeing mental resources for higher-level thinking and problem solving. Research shows that when students achieve automaticity in basic skills like arithmetic, they can better focus on understanding and tackling more complex mathematical concepts and applications (Sweller, 2011). This shift enables students to engage in deeper learning and reasoning, which is essential for mastering advanced topics. For instance, when students can effortlessly multiply or add numbers, they can better focus on solving complex algebraic equations or understanding geometric proofs.

Critically, the CMC framework addresses the coexistence and interwoven nature of automaticity and problem-solving capabilities. This integration is pivotal because it allows students to effortlessly perform basic calculations, which in turn enables them to more deeply engage with challenging conceptual problems. The framework not only fosters quick computational skills but integrates these skills with strategic and conceptual competencies necessary for solving real-world problems. This approach ensures that students are proficient in executing calculations and also adept at applying these skills within broader mathematical reasoning and problem-solving contexts. The aim is to ensure that students are not bogged down by the mechanics of computation when they should be navigating higher-level mathematical thinking and problem-solving scenarios.

These key principles are integral to balancing the development of automaticity and problem-solving skills within the CMC framework.

By structuring instructional activities that integrate fluency practice with meaningful problem-solving tasks, teachers can help students develop both speed and depth in their mathematical thinking. The following items represent core strategies for achieving this balance.

- **Integrated instructional approaches:** Teaching practices should simultaneously develop automaticity in basic operations and engage students in activities that require substantial problem solving. For example, while students practice multiplication facts to develop fluency, they should also solve problems that involve applying these facts in various scenarios, such as in geometry or data analysis.

- **Cumulative learning experiences:** Design learning experiences that build on existing knowledge. As students become more automatic in certain skills, introduce more complex problems that challenge them to apply their skills in new and varied contexts.

- **Reflective and adaptive learning:** Encourage students to reflect on how they use basic skills in problem solving. This reflection can help them understand how foundational skills support more complex mathematical thinking and how these elements are interdependent.

Educators play a critical role in balancing the development of automaticity and problem-solving skills. They must craft learning environments that value the quick and efficient execution of mathematical operations while also deeply valuing the exploration and application of mathematics and mathematics' connection to real-life problems. Educators should clearly explain why both speed in certain skills and depth of understanding are necessary to help students see the practical and theoretical importance of each.

By addressing the misconception that speed alone equates to mathematical competence and articulating the importance of procedural fluency and automaticity in conjunction with robust problem solving within the CMC framework, teachers can pave the way for a more comprehensive, effective, and nuanced approach to mathematics education. Lessons should integrate fluency with opportunities to explore and apply mathematical concepts in various contexts. This balanced focus prepares students for academic success with mathematical procedures; helps them know when, why, and where to apply these procedures; and equips them with the critical thinking and problem-solving skills necessary for lifelong learning and application in a complex world.

In designing classroom tasks within the CMC framework, teachers must establish a structured relationship between developing quick computation skills and promoting deep conceptual understanding. Tasks should be diverse and enriching, organized in such a way that they give students opportunities to practice fluency while simultaneously challenging them to apply their knowledge in new and unfamiliar contexts. For instance, a mathematics teacher might employ a project-based learning approach in which students use their arithmetic skills to plan a community garden, calculate costs, and analyze growth patterns. This structured integration of procedural fluency and conceptual understanding is a central element of the conceptual and procedural integration competency within the CMC framework.

Encouraging Constructive Challenge

Encouraging constructive challenge is essential in the mathematics classroom. This concept goes beyond mere difficulty; it involves designing tasks that push students' current understanding while providing the necessary support to ensure meaningful growth. Constructive challenge allows students to engage deeply with the material, apply their knowledge in new contexts, and reflect on strategies for overcoming obstacles. This process fosters resilience and a deep understanding of mathematical concepts.

Many educators have traditionally embraced the growth mindset (the belief that effort leads to success), but research suggests that growth mindset interventions alone do not significantly enhance mathematical achievement. Studies by Li and Bates (2020) and Yeager and colleagues (2019) indicate that although promoting a growth mindset can have positive effects, these interventions, when used in isolation, yield minimal gains in mathematics. Instead, the most effective way to improve achievement is through explicit skill-building instruction (Fuchs, Newman-Gonchar, et al., 2021). Therefore, while it's important to nurture perseverance, constructive challenge focuses on building the foundational skills for students to effectively navigate challenges.

This approach aligns with research on desirable difficulty—tasks that are challenging yet attainable given the student's current skill level. Similarly, L. S. Vygotsky's (1978) zone of proximal development highlights that students learn best when they receive tasks just beyond their independent ability but within reach with appropriate guidance. Constructive challenge places students in this optimal learning zone, ensuring that their struggle leads to growth rather than frustration.

Teachers play a pivotal role in creating environments where constructive challenge thrives. Research by Codding and colleagues (2017) shows that setting clear learning goals, offering specific feedback, and giving students opportunities to reflect on their progress foster persistence through challenges. These strategies help students navigate difficult tasks and understand that effort paired with skill building leads to mastery.

It is equally important to appropriately scaffold tasks so that students have mastered basic skills before engaging with more complex problems. The National Council of Teachers of Mathematics (2014) advocates for balancing skill development with opportunities for exploration, ensuring that students can engage with problems in meaningful ways without becoming overwhelmed.

Ultimately, constructive challenge shifts the focus from struggle for its own sake to struggle with a clear purpose. It involves the strategic use of difficulty to build competence, increase engagement, and support long-term growth in mathematics. By fostering this environment, teachers empower students to approach challenges with confidence, knowing they have the tools to succeed.

The Role of Educators in Shaping Mathematical Mindsets

Teachers hold a crucial role in shaping students' attitudes toward mathematics. Through this framework, teachers can employ strategies that foster a positive, inclusive, and deeply understanding-focused approach to mathematics education. By transforming students' perceptions of mathematics from a daunting obstacle to an engaging and surmountable challenge, teachers are pivotal in reshaping how students interact with and perceive the subject. This transformation involves promoting a mindset that embraces challenges, values persistent effort, and views mistakes as essential learning opportunities. The CMC framework emphasizes the integration of strands such as procedural fluency and conceptual understanding with adaptive reasoning and elements like problem-solving skills. This structured approach ensures that students are becoming proficient in mathematical techniques and also developing the skills necessary to creatively and effectively apply these techniques in diverse situations.

Moreover, by fostering a supportive learning environment that encourages constructive challenge and exploration, teachers help cultivate a generation of learners who approach mathematical problems with curiosity, resilience, and confidence. These qualities are invaluable, extending beyond the mathematics classroom. The impact of this shift transcends improving academic outcomes; it nurtures a holistic educational experience that equips students with a robust mathematical mindset. Such a mindset is critical in today's world where mathematics is not just a subject to be learned but a vital and empowering tool for problem solving and critical thinking in various real-world contexts.

Therefore, in the CMC framework, the role of the teacher extends from instructor to mentor and facilitator, guiding students through a journey of mathematical discovery and growth. Through their implementation of a structured, competency-based approach, teachers develop both proficient mathematicians and well-rounded, resilient individuals.

Conclusion

Persistent misconceptions about mathematics education shape how teachers instruct and how students engage with mathematical content. Addressing these misconceptions is not just a preliminary step—it is essential groundwork for implementing the CMC framework. By confronting and debunking common myths about learning mathematics, educators can better prepare themselves to adopt new strategies that promote deeper understanding, meaningful problem solving, and long-term student engagement.

The transition from a mindset focused solely on procedural fluency to one that embraces the broader scope of mathematics learning is key to ensuring that students are proficient in calculations as well as truly empowered to understand and apply mathematics in diverse contexts. As we move forward, we must shed old beliefs about inherent ability, memorization, and the speed of learning, replacing them with practices rooted in the evidence that conceptual understanding, fluency, and reasoning are interconnected.

In the remaining chapters, we'll explore how each competency within the CMC framework addresses these needs, providing actionable strategies that empower educators to foster a holistic, meaningful, and enriched mathematical learning experience for all students. The following questions are designed to help you reflect on this chapter's content as you progress through this book.

1. How do misconceptions about mathematics learning affect your current instructional practices?
2. What steps can you take to challenge and dispel these myths within your classroom or school community?
3. How might addressing these misconceptions influence the way your students perceive and engage with mathematics?
4. In what ways can the CMC framework help you build a more comprehensive and integrated approach to teaching mathematics?

CHAPTER 2

Conceptual and Procedural Integration

The CMC framework emphasizes the integration of conceptual understanding and procedural fluency as foundational to effective mathematics education. Indeed, this vital competency bridges the gap between understanding the why behind mathematical concepts and mastering the how of applying them through procedural techniques. In this chapter, we'll delve into the dynamic interplay of these two strands or elements, illustrating how their integration enriches learning and also enhances flexibility and precision in mathematical problem solving. Let's first take a look at the essence of conceptual and procedural integration before exploring its efficacy and related research and, finally, strategies to enhance conceptual and procedural integration.

The Essence of Conceptual and Procedural Integration

Our exploration of the CMC framework competencies begins with the idea that conceptual understanding and procedural fluency are not mutually exclusive but interdependent, a notion that both educators and students must ultimately internalize. *Conceptual understanding* in mathematics extends beyond knowing isolated facts and methods—it involves a deep and integrated grasp of why mathematical concepts are important and how they apply in various contexts. *Procedural fluency* is an integral strand of mathematical proficiency, encompassing the ability to carry out mathematical procedures and know when and how to apply these procedures in different contexts. Integrating the two, then, equips students to see beyond mere formulas and algorithms and delve into the foundational principles that govern their application. Such an understanding fosters deeper engagement with the material, as students learn to perform calculations and also to appreciate the reasoning that underpins these procedures. Before we dig deeper into the integration of these strands or elements, let's take the time to zero in on each of them.

Conceptual Understanding

When you foster conceptual understanding—a thorough understanding of the why of mathematical concepts and how the concepts apply in various contexts—you allow students to see connections between and among different ideas, which facilitates acquisition of new knowledge by linking it to what students already know. These connections not only aid learning but also significantly enhance students' ability to retain and recall information. Students are less likely to forget or misconstrue a mathematical concept when they deeply understand it.

Consider, for example, how two different students might approach dividing fractions. A student with surface-level understanding might simply memorize the "flip and multiply" algorithm without understanding why it works. When faced with a problem like $\frac{3}{4} \div \frac{1}{2}$, they mechanically invert the second fraction and multiply: $\frac{3}{4} \times \frac{2}{1}$. While they may arrive at the correct answer of $\frac{3}{2}$, they might struggle to explain what this answer means or why the procedure works.

In contrast, a student with conceptual understanding would recognize that dividing by $\frac{1}{2}$ means finding how many halves are contained in $\frac{3}{4}$. They might reason that since each half is $\frac{2}{4}$, and they have $\frac{3}{4}$, they have $1\frac{1}{2}$ or $\frac{3}{2}$. This deeper understanding allows them to do the following.

- Visualize the problem using models or diagrams.
- Explain why the algorithm works.
- Apply this understanding to solve related problems.
- Recognize when their answer makes sense in context.

This example illustrates how conceptual understanding goes beyond knowing how to perform a procedure to understanding why it works and when to apply it—knowledge that supports both retention and flexible application.

For you as an educator, promoting conceptual understanding means encouraging students to actively engage with the material. This involves guiding them to monitor their own comprehension and adjust their learning approaches as needed. If a particular method or concept doesn't make sense to a student, urge them to explore it further, discuss it with peers, or seek clarification. This active involvement in their learning process enhances their ability to apply mathematical concepts flexibly and creatively, which is crucial for solving complex problems in academic settings and in everyday life. Furthermore, teaching strategies that foster conceptual understanding should give students opportunities to explore mathematical ideas through multiple representations and contexts. This approach helps cement their knowledge and skills across various situations and encourages them to form a coherent picture of mathematical concepts. As students progress in their mathematics education, this foundation of understanding not only prepares them for more advanced topics but also instills a lifelong appreciation and curiosity for the subject. A student with a robust conceptual understanding of multiplication understands it as an array or repeated addition, which aids them in visualizing multiplication facts and applying those facts to such tasks as calculating area or understanding algebraic expressions. This foundational understanding is crucial for engaging with more complex mathematical ideas and for fostering a genuine interest in mathematics as a logical and interconnected system.

Looking at the development of conceptual understanding in greater detail, it's useful to consider two practical aspects: (1) the importance of multiple representations and (2) the role of knowledge clusters.

The Importance of Multiple Representations

A fundamental aspect of developing conceptual understanding in mathematics is students' ability to utilize and transition between multiple representations of mathematical ideas. Research by Powell and colleagues (2020) demonstrates that successful mathematics interventions consistently incorporate multiple representations to build robust understanding. This finding is further supported by Fuchs, Newman-Gonchar, and colleagues (2021), whose research shows that students achieve better outcomes when instruction systematically connects different representations of mathematical concepts. This skill is critical, as it enriches students' understanding and provides flexibility in how they approach and solve problems. The various representations—whether visual, numerical, symbolic, or contextual—serve as different lenses through which students can examine and make sense of mathematical concepts. Understanding the interconnections among these representations deepens students' grasp and allows for more robust engagement with the material.

The incorporation of multiple representations aligns with findings from Rittle-Johnson (2017), who emphasizes that deep mathematical understanding develops through opportunities to see and work with concepts in various forms. When students can move flexibly between different representations, they develop more complete and transferable mathematical knowledge.

For instance, consider solving for an unknown variable in a simple algebraic equation, such as $x + 4 = 9$. Students might begin by using physical objects like counters to represent the equation, showing 4 counters plus a mystery number of counters that together equal 9. This concrete representation helps them visualize the problem. They might then create a number line, using a jump from 4 to 9 to represent adding x. This visual approach shows the concept of "solving for x" as finding the distance needed to reach 9 from 4. In a more symbolic representation, students might isolate x by subtracting 4 from both sides of the equation, demonstrating an understanding of maintaining equality.

Through such activities, you can guide students to discuss and reflect on how different representations help solve the problem, what the strengths and limitations of each are, and why they must align to achieve consistent results. This discussion promotes critical thinking and helps students appreciate the utility of diverse mathematical representations. Research by Schneider and colleagues (2011) demonstrates that students who can flexibly select and use different representations develop greater mathematical competence and problem-solving capabilities. Powell and colleagues (2020) find that effective mathematics instruction explicitly teaches students how to choose and use appropriate representations, leading to improved mathematical outcomes. As students become more adept at using various representations, they also become more proficient in choosing the most effective representation based on the context of the problem. This selection process is vital for their future mathematical competence, as Rittle-Johnson and Schneider (2015) show that the ability to strategically select and use different representations is a key indicator of mathematical proficiency and predicts success with more complex mathematical tasks.

Moreover, teaching that emphasizes the links among different representations can illuminate the structure of mathematics, revealing it as a web rather than a series of isolated topics. This knowledge is crucial for students to feel confident navigating the mathematical terrain. Thus, as educators, we must provide varied opportunities for students to engage with multiple forms of mathematical representations and encourage them to make connections between these forms. This approach not only enhances their immediate problem-solving skills but also contributes to a deeper, more enduring understanding of mathematics. As we proceed, we will explore specific strategies and classroom activities that can help facilitate this kind of rich, interconnected mathematics learning.

The Role of Knowledge Clusters

The concept of conceptual understanding in mathematics encompasses students' ability to organize their knowledge into efficient and interconnected clusters. These clusters, which may be summarized by succinct phrases or concepts such as *properties of multiplication*, serve to reduce cognitive load and to help students recognize structural similarities across different mathematical contexts. This organization of knowledge into compact clusters enables students to efficiently apply learned principles to a variety of seemingly unrelated problems, effectively reducing the amount of "new" learning required for each situation.

These knowledge clusters are not static; they can be dynamically unpacked when necessary. For instance, a student may recall the general properties of multiplication for quick problem-solving or routine tasks. However, when faced with a novel situation in which deeper reflection or explanation is required, the student may delve deeper into the cluster to explore and articulate specific principles or concepts. This ability to toggle between compact and expanded views of knowledge is crucial for adapting to new learning situations and for explaining complex ideas to others.

Furthermore, conceptual understanding in mathematics often manifests in a hierarchical form. Simpler clusters of ideas are nested within larger, more complex structures, allowing for a systematic exploration of mathematical concepts. For example, the concept of a number line serves as a fundamental cluster that younger students might initially see as a tool for understanding basic arithmetic operations. Initially, it may represent basic positive integers, but gradually, it encompasses rational numbers and, later, real numbers and beyond. It illustrates the operations of arithmetic geometrically, such as representing addition and subtraction through spatial movements along the line. As students advance in their mathematics education, this same number line evolves into a more comprehensive tool that integrates their understanding of arithmetic, geometry, number systems, and algebra, perhaps representing inequalities or visualizing functions.

The integration of arithmetic with geometry through a number line also paves the way for more advanced mathematical studies. For older students, it becomes a foundation for exploring limits and continuity in calculus or for understanding vectors and coordinate systems in higher mathematics. The number line, therefore, serves not only as a practical tool for solving problems but also as a conceptual bridge connecting different mathematical disciplines. While mathematics education pioneer Richard R. Skemp (1978) first established the importance of relational understanding in mathematics, research has since substantially reinforced Skemp's finding. Michael Schneider and Elsbeth Stern (2010) demonstrate through their multimethod studies that such integrated understanding of mathematical representations supports flexible problem solving across contexts. This finding is further supported by Rittle-Johnson's (2017) research showing that when students develop deep conceptual connections between mathematical representations, they become more adept at transferring their knowledge to new mathematical domains. Additionally, Powell and colleagues (2020) find that successful mathematics interventions consistently emphasize these conceptual bridges between different mathematical representations and domains, leading to more robust and transferable mathematical understanding.

By fostering an environment where students can develop and manipulate such hierarchical knowledge clusters, educators support current learning objectives, enable students to build robust understanding, and equip students with the cognitive tools necessary for future mathematical challenges. Emphasizing and expanding on these interconnected knowledge clusters within your teaching practices can significantly enhance students' mathematical proficiency and their ability to apply mathematical concepts across diverse and advanced domains.

Procedural Fluency

As mentioned earlier, procedural fluency involves not just carrying out mathematical procedures but knowing when and how to apply them in different contexts. It's a strand or element that includes performing mathematical tasks with flexibility, accuracy, and efficiency, qualities that are essential for effective problem solving and mathematical reasoning. In the domain of numbers, procedural fluency supports and enriches conceptual understanding, particularly in the areas of place value and the properties and operations of rational numbers. For example, a strong grasp of procedural skills helps students understand why certain algorithms work for addition, subtraction, multiplication, and division, which facilitates a deeper conceptual understanding of these operations. This dual strength allows students to move beyond rote calculation to make meaningful connections between different mathematical ideas.

Procedural fluency also plays a critical role in analyzing the similarities and differences between various calculation methods. This analysis is not limited to traditional written methods; it includes mental mathematics strategies and the use of digital and physical tools such as calculators, computers, and manipulatives like blocks and beads. Each method offers unique advantages that can be leveraged in different situations. For instance, mental mathematics is invaluable for quick estimates and checks, while physical tools are especially helpful in illustrating abstract concepts to provide a concrete basis for understanding.

The use of technology and manipulatives in teaching mathematical procedures has expanded the repertoire of methods available to students and educators. Calculators and computers, for example, can quickly and accurately handle complex computations, allowing students to focus on higher-order-thinking skills such as problem solving and analysis. Meanwhile, manipulatives offer a hands-on way to explore and internalize mathematical concepts, bridging the gap between concrete experiences and abstract reasoning.

Furthermore, procedural fluency facilitates the exploration of multiple solution paths, which encourages students to compare and choose the most effective strategy based on the problem context. This ability to select and use an appropriate method enhances students' mathematical agility and confidence. For instance, when faced with a complex division problem, a student with high procedural fluency might choose

Conceptual and Procedural Integration　33

to use a calculator in a test scenario to ensure accuracy but might use long division in a teaching setting to demonstrate the process to peers.

Educators help students develop procedural fluency by giving them varied opportunities to practice and apply different mathematical procedures in meaningful contexts. This involves teaching procedures' steps and discussing their uses, advantages, and limitations. Such discussions help students understand the why behind the how, simultaneously reinforcing their conceptual understanding and procedural skills.

Ultimately, procedural fluency is about more than just getting the right answer—it's about understanding the processes that lead to that answer and being able to apply them in flexible and thoughtful ways.

Competency Integration

By fostering both procedural fluency and conceptual understanding, educators can help students build a robust mathematical foundation that supports a wide range of cognitive and practical skills, and therefore prepares them for complex problem solving and decision making in academic and real-world settings. But crucially, competency integration is key to transformative instruction and learning. A lack of competency integration may result in fraught, compartmentalized learning.

Studies by Rittle-Johnson (2017) demonstrate that when students learn mathematical skills in isolation without foundational understanding, they often struggle to see connections between different mathematical concepts, making it more difficult for them to grasp new topics. Powell and colleagues (2020) find through their synthesis of mathematics interventions that this lack of interconnected knowledge leads to a fragmented approach to learning, where each new problem may seem to require a unique procedural method. This compartmentalization is particularly evident in early education, as documented by Nelson and McMaster's (2019) meta-analysis of early numeracy interventions, which shows how disconnected instruction can impede mathematical development. A student may learn one method for addition problems, like 305 + 597, using standard algorithms, and a completely different strategy for adding numbers when the sum exceeds a ten or a hundred, like 999 + 244.

Such compartmentalized learning not only makes mathematical thinking rigid but also restricts students' ability to relate school-based learning with real-world applications. For many students, a clear dichotomy emerges: They see the problem-solving methods they use in school as separate from and unrelated to those they use in everyday life. This separation significantly limits their ability to employ mathematical thinking in practical, real-life problem-solving scenarios.

Furthermore, when students learn procedures without a deeper understanding, they often lack the flexibility to adapt or simplify these procedures based on the context. Conversely, students who understand the underlying principles of mathematics are better equipped to manipulate and adjust procedures to make problem solving more efficient. For example, consider a student faced with the problem of subtracting 198 from 457. A student who takes a procedural approach might use a standard subtraction algorithm. In contrast, a student who understands the relationships between numbers might adjust these numbers to make the problem simpler, such as rounding 198 to 200, subtracting to get 257, and then adding back 2 to get the final result of 259. Moreover, students with a strong conceptual foundation are capable of using flexible strategies across various settings, not just in classroom tasks but in everyday calculations. For instance, in quickly calculating a 20 percent tip, a student might round $23.76 to $24.00 for simplicity, calculate 10 percent of $24.00 as $2.40, and then double it to get $4.80, rather than directly dealing with the more cumbersome original amount.

To encourage a more integrated and flexible approach to mathematics learning, educators should focus on building a robust network of concepts that students can draw on. You can achieve this by emphasizing relational understanding alongside procedural training. When introducing new mathematical operations, for example, explicitly linking them to previously learned concepts can help students see the broader mathematical landscape rather than viewing each new topic as an isolated island of knowledge. For instance, when teaching

Conceptual and Procedural Integration

the algorithm for long division, you must connect it to the concept of division as repeated subtraction. You could demonstrate this by dividing a large quantity of objects into smaller groups and showing how the algorithm simplifies this process. A practical classroom task could have students use manipulatives to divide sets of objects and then transition to the abstract algorithm, noting each step's purpose and its relationship to the manipulative activity. This method solidifies the conceptual basis for the procedure while enhancing procedural fluency.

>
> **Task example:** Conceptual-to-procedural transition
>
> **Manipulative activity:** First-grade students use blocks to divide a set of 24 into groups of 4, discussing with partners how many groups they can make.
>
> **Transition to algorithm:** Fifth-grade students replicate the manipulative division using the long division algorithm, identifying how each step of the algorithm corresponds to the action of dividing the blocks.

By fostering an environment where students understand the why and the how of mathematics, we equip them to academically succeed and to effectively apply their knowledge outside of school. This approach enriches students' mathematical experiences and prepares them to confidently and creatively tackle a wide range of problems in later education pursuits and everyday life.

The integration of conceptual understanding and procedural fluency is not merely a pedagogical recommendation—it is a necessity for developing mathematical proficiency. This method of teaching adheres to the principles outlined by researchers and aligns with best practices that emphasize understanding's importance in learning, making mathematics more accessible and meaningful for all students.

The Power of Integrated Mathematics Learning

The integration of conceptual understanding and procedural fluency we've explored—from multiple representations to interconnected knowledge—is not just theoretically sound but empirically validated.

Extensive research demonstrates how this balanced approach enhances students' mathematical proficiency in measurable ways. Studies consistently show that students who develop strong conceptual foundations alongside procedural fluency are better able to transfer knowledge to new contexts and perform effectively on mathematical tasks.

According to Rittle-Johnson (2017), students with deep conceptual knowledge can flexibly apply what they know to solve novel problems, a key indicator of mathematical proficiency. This finding is reinforced by Powell and colleagues (2020), whose synthesis of mathematics interventions demonstrates that this type of integrated understanding supports students in effortlessly carrying out mathematical procedures, which in turn frees their cognitive resources for more complex problem solving and analysis. Research by Fuchs, Wang, and colleagues (2021) further underscores the significance of an integrated approach to teaching mathematics, showing through randomized controlled trials that when conceptual understanding and procedural knowledge are intertwined, students achieve significantly better outcomes. This method fosters more meaningful learning outcomes by allowing students to comprehend not just how to perform mathematical operations but also why these operations function as they do. Such an understanding deepens students' mathematical reasoning and prepares them for more complex problem-solving scenarios. By grasping the rationale behind mathematical procedures, students are likely to retain the knowledge longer and apply it more effectively in diverse contexts, leading to more durable and meaningful learning outcomes.

Studies highlight that integrating conceptual and procedural knowledge supports deeper learning and application. For example, educational psychology research by Bethany Rittle-Johnson, Michael Schneider, and Jon R. Star (2015) emphasizes that students who concurrently develop procedural skills and conceptual understanding achieve higher levels of overall mathematical proficiency. Their study reveals that students who are taught these skills together perform better on assessments and show greater ability to transfer this knowledge to different contexts (Rittle-Johnson et al., 2015).

Another significant contribution comes from Schneider and Stern (2010), whose work investigates how students' conceptual and procedural knowledge development impacts their problem-solving abilities. They report that an integrated approach helps students see the connections between mathematical concepts and processes, which facilitates a smoother transition and application of knowledge across different mathematical topics and real-world scenarios.

Another study by educational researchers Emily R. Fyfe, Percival G. Matthews, Eric Amsel, Katherine L. McEldoon, and Nicole M. McNeil (2018) offers additional support for the integrated approach to teaching mathematics. Their research specifically explores the synergy between conceptual knowledge and procedural fluency in elementary school students' learning about fractions. The study demonstrates that students who engage in instruction that explicitly connects procedural practices with conceptual understanding not only improve in their immediate handling of fractions but also develop a better foundational grasp of the subject. This deeper understanding enables them to more adeptly apply their knowledge in unfamiliar problem contexts and to sustain their learning over time. Fyfe and colleagues (2018) use a method that actively involves students in discovering the reasons behind the procedures they learn, such as why certain methods for adding fractions work. The researchers find that this method of instruction leads to significant gains in the depth and the flexibility of students' mathematical understanding (Fyfe et al., 2018). Incorporating findings from Fyfe and colleagues (2018) into instructional practices can be particularly effective in topics like fractions, where students often struggle to see the connection between procedural methods and underlying concepts. By focusing on these connections, educators can help students build a more comprehensive and durable mathematical tool kit.

These studies underscore the importance of instructional strategies that do not isolate skill development and conceptual understanding but rather intertwine them. Such research encourages educators to employ teaching methods that promote an understanding of why mathematical procedures work in the way they do. They can achieve this through practical activities that connect mathematical concepts with real-life applications, visual and interactive technology that illustrates abstract concepts, and discussions or prompts that encourage students to reflect on their mathematical thinking. By valuing both procedural skills and conceptual insights in the classroom, educators can provide students with a robust framework for understanding mathematics. This improves their immediate problem-solving capabilities and also builds a strong foundation for their future academic and professional endeavors, enhancing their ability to use mathematical knowledge creatively and effectively across various situations. This integrated approach, therefore, facilitates immediate academic success as well as prepares students for lifelong engagement with mathematics.

This chapter next outlines strategies and tasks designed to foster this integration, ensuring that students learn mathematical procedures and also deeply understand the concepts that underpin them.

Strategies to Enhance Conceptual and Procedural Integration

In the CMC framework, I prioritize the seamless integration of conceptual understanding and procedural fluency to cultivate students' deep mathematical skills. The strategies in this section aim to capture the crucial synergy between ensuring students grasp the mathematical operations behind the procedures and equipping them with the practical abilities to apply these procedures effectively.

For instance, a conceptual and procedural integration approach to teaching multiplication would not only teach students how to multiply numbers but also explore the concept of multiplication as repeated addition. A practical classroom activity might have students use arrays or group objects to visually represent and solve multiplication problems, such as determining the total number of objects in several groups of the same size. This visual representation helps students understand why multiplication works and how it relates to addition, enhancing their ability to grasp more abstract concepts as they progress.

Further, when students learn about fractions, they should understand why certain procedures for adding fractions are necessary—such as finding a common denominator—before mechanically applying these procedures. A task might involve comparing fractions using different methods, such as using fraction strips to visually demonstrate why $\frac{1}{3}$ is larger than $\frac{1}{4}$, and then moving on to the procedural skill of converting these fractions to have a common denominator for addition. This both reinforces the procedure and deepens understanding by linking it to a tangible concept.

In geometry, teaching the formula for the area of a rectangle (length × width) can be enriched by having students first explore the concept by tiling rectangles on graph paper and counting the unit squares, thus visually demonstrating why the formula works. This approach solidifies both the conceptual understanding of area as a measure of space and the procedural method for calculating it.

To further illustrate how this integration plays out, let's thoroughly examine examples from elementary, middle, and high school classrooms. These examples will show how the same underlying principles of conceptual and procedural integration are adapted to suit the cognitive and developmental stages of students. Each example demonstrates specific mathematical procedures as well as aligns with pedagogical strategies designed to deepen students' understanding and facilitate their ability to apply mathematical concepts independently and creatively. This approach aligns with research that highlights the importance of connecting conceptual knowledge with procedural skills to enhance problem-solving capabilities and mathematical reasoning. Let's delve into these scenarios to see how conceptual and procedural integration can be effectively implemented across the spectrum of K–12 mathematics classrooms.

The effective integration of conceptual understanding and procedural fluency requires systematic implementation across all grade levels. While the specific content and complexity may vary, three fundamental strategies remain consistent throughout mathematics education: (1) building strong conceptual foundations, (2) developing systematic procedural fluency, and (3) creating meaningful connections between concepts and procedures. Each strategy manifests differently at elementary, middle, and high school levels (exemplified in the following sections), but the underlying principles remain the same. These grade-level examples demonstrate how teachers can implement these strategies to support students' mathematical development, showing both the progression of mathematical thinking and the consistent need for balanced instruction. By examining how these strategies unfold across different grade levels, teachers can better understand how to effectively adapt and apply them in their own classrooms.

Conceptual Understanding

At the elementary level, students begin their mathematical journey by exploring addition and subtraction through engaging and interactive methods. Initially, teachers introduce these concepts using visual aids such as number lines and tactile tools like block manipulatives.

> To solve the problem 8 + 7, students might use blocks to physically group 8 and 7 units together, observing the combined total. Similarly, for 15 − 9, students could start with a group of 15 blocks and physically remove 9 to see what remains. This method helps them conceptualize addition as the combination of quantities and subtraction as the separation of quantities.

Teachers often use stories or real-life scenarios that require combining or separating objects, which contextualizes these operations within students' everyday experiences. Such strategies emphasize understanding the meaning behind addition and subtraction, rather than relying solely on rote memorization.

In middle school, students deepen their understanding of fractions and ratios, exploring these concepts as fundamental tools for comparing and quantifying relationships.

> Fractions are introduced as parts of a whole, where students visualize and manipulate segments of shapes (like pies or bars) to understand how a fraction represents a division of any whole

into equal parts. Students explore various representations of fractions, such as on a number line or through pie charts, to see how fractions like $\frac{1}{2}$ or $\frac{3}{4}$ depict parts of a single entity.

Ratios are introduced as a means to compare two quantities, emphasizing their role in expressing the relative sizes of two measures. Students engage in activities such as comparing the number of red marbles and the number of blue marbles in a bag or comparing the speeds of two runners. They learn to see ratios as both fractional comparisons and part-to-part and part-to-whole formats, which aids them in understanding proportional relationships and their practical applications, such as in maps or models.

In high school algebra, students explore the foundational concept of variables as representations of unknown quantities that vary within mathematical relationships. This understanding is crucial for grasping more complex topics such as functions, equations, and inequalities.

Students learn that algebraic expressions and equations model real-world situations and that solving these equations involves finding the values of variables that make the equations true.

Students also delve into functions, understanding them as mathematical entities that assign each input exactly one output. This concept is expanded to different types of functions, such as linear, quadratic, and exponential, all characterized by specific patterns and properties. Conceptually, students explore how changes in the input of a function affect the output, helping them understand the rate of change, intercepts, and overall behavior of functions graphically and algebraically.

Procedural Fluency

As students' understanding of concepts deepens, the focus gradually shifts toward developing procedural fluency.

Introduce elementary students to the standard algorithms for addition and subtraction, which are systematic methods for handling larger numbers. Through repeated practice, they learn the steps involved in these algorithms, such as carrying over in addition when the sum exceeds 10 or borrowing in subtraction when the top digit is smaller than the bottom digit. This practice includes structured exercises that guide students through each step of the process, ensuring they grasp the purpose and mechanics of carrying and borrowing. Reinforce these algorithms by having students solve problems both with and without manipulatives, bridging the gap between concrete experiences and abstract procedures.

As students' conceptual grasp strengthens in middle school, they learn the procedural skills needed to mathematically manipulate fractions and ratios.

For fractions, this includes operations like adding fractions with like denominators by simply adding the numerators or adding fractions with unlike denominators by finding a common denominator first. Students also tackle more complex operations like multiplying and dividing fractions, understanding these operations in terms of repeated addition and the inverse of multiplication, respectively.

For ratios, procedural fluency involves solving problems that require converting ratios to fractions to simplify comparisons, or scaling ratios up or down to create equivalent ratios, crucial for tasks like resizing images or creating scale models. For instance, if a scale model uses the ratio 1:50, students learn to apply this ratio to convert actual measurements into model dimensions and vice versa.

And in high school, students develop procedural fluency by learning to manipulate algebraic expressions and efficiently solve equations. This includes skills like simplifying expressions, solving linear and quadratic equations, and working with inequalities.

In solving the quadratic equation $ax^2 + bx + c = 0$, students apply the quadratic formula, understanding each component of the formula and how it derives from completing the square.

Procedural practice also involves solving systems of equations, where students use methods such as substitution, elimination, and graphical analysis. These techniques require a precise understanding of how equations interact and how solutions can be interpreted in terms of intersections of lines or curves on a graph.

Integration in Teaching

To effectively integrate conceptual understanding with procedural fluency, teachers employ a variety of instructional strategies that connect tangible activities with abstract algorithms.

> In elementary school with addition and subtraction, in exploring the problem 8 + 7, you might first have students use blocks to build two sets, count them together, and then transition to representing the same problem on a number line. Following these concrete representations, you then guide students to solve the same problem using the traditional addition algorithm.

This multimodal approach not only solidifies the students' understanding of the operations but also shows them how different methods are interconnected and lead to the same result. Furthermore, encourage students to explain their reasoning in each method, discussing how moving blocks or jumping spaces on a number line correlates to the steps in the algorithm. This holistic approach helps students see the mathematical operations as both practical and applicable to various situations, enhancing their overall mathematical literacy and confidence.

To effectively integrate these concepts and procedures, teachers often present real-world scenarios that require conceptual understanding and procedural skills. A common application for middle school students is adjusting recipes, which naturally combine fractions and ratios.

> Present a cookie recipe that requires 2 cups of flour for 24 cookies, and ask students to adjust the recipe to make 60 cookies. Students must first understand the ratio involved (flour to cookies) and then use their skills with fractions to determine the new quantity of flour needed, multiplying the original fraction (2 cups for 24 cookies) by the factor that scales 24 cookies up to 60.

> Another integration approach is a project like creating scale drawings or models. You might task students with designing a miniature garden where they need to apply their understanding of scale and proportion using ratios. They calculate real-world measurements of garden elements (like paths or beds) and then use ratios to create a scaled model, applying their fractional and ratio calculations to ensure accuracy and fidelity to scale.

In both cases, teachers guide students to not only perform calculations but also articulate their understanding of how the mathematical procedures apply to the problem at hand. This deepens their conceptual grasp while enhancing their procedural fluency, preparing them for more complex applications of mathematics in academic and real-life situations.

To integrate conceptual understanding with procedural fluency in high school algebra, you can employ tasks that contextualize algebraic techniques within real-world problems.

> Ask students to solve a problem involving profit maximization where they need to determine the price at which the profit, modeled by the quadratic equation $P(x) = -5x^2 + 150x - 1,000$, is maximized. Here, students would use differentiation to find the vertex of the parabola, applying both algebraic skills and an understanding of the function's graph.
>
> You can also integrate the use of technology, such as graphing calculators or algebraic software, to allow students to visualize algebraic equations and their solutions. For instance, plotting the graph of $y = mx + b$ helps students see the impact of changes in slope (m) and y-intercept (b) on the line's position and steepness, connecting the equation's algebraic manipulation with its graphical representation.

This approach helps students see algebra not just as a set of rules to follow but as a powerful tool for modeling and solving practical problems, reinforcing algebra's relevance to real life and other areas of mathematics. It encourages deeper engagement with the subject, where students apply algebraic thinking to novel situations, fostering both a solid understanding of core concepts and the ability to use algebraic methods creatively and effectively.

Conclusion

In this chapter, we've explored the indispensable integration of conceptual understanding and procedural fluency within the CMC framework. This synthesis is foundational for fostering effective mathematics education that enriches learning as well as enhances flexibility and precision in mathematical problem solving. Deep conceptual knowledge empowers students to understand the why and how of mathematics, enabling them to connect and integrate new knowledge with what they already know. Procedural fluency complements this by providing the skills necessary to efficiently and accurately execute mathematical procedures. The integration of these strands or elements allows students to navigate the terrain of mathematics with confidence and agility. It prepares them to tackle complex problems by applying a blend of conceptual understanding and procedural skill, thus bridging the gap between theoretical knowledge and practical application.

It is our responsibility as educators to foster environments that cultivate this dual competency, enabling students to develop a holistic understanding of mathematics—and research supports this integrated approach. The studies I've mentioned provide empirical evidence that an integrated approach enhances immediate learning outcomes and equips students with the skills to adapt and apply their knowledge in varied contexts. As we move forward, we must continue exploring and implementing strategies that integrate these strands or elements throughout teaching practices. By doing so, we enhance individual learning outcomes and also contribute to broader understanding and appreciation of mathematics as a dynamic and integral part of human knowledge; students can truly appreciate the beauty of mathematics and its relevance to the world, equipped with the skills necessary to explore, discover, and innovate. As we continue to develop and refine our teaching methods, let us strive to foster both the curiosity to question and the skill to solve, building a foundation that supports academic success and lifelong engagement with mathematics.

CHAPTER 3

Problem Solving and Modeling

The core component of problem solving and modeling marks a significant departure from traditional approaches to mathematics education, which often emphasize rote memorization. Shifting instead to a dynamic, application-oriented understanding of mathematics, this approach engages students with real-world challenges that demand knowledge as well as creativity, strategic thinking, and the capacity to model various scenarios mathematically. Problem solving in mathematics involves the ability to formulate, represent, and solve mathematical problems, and to create models that simulate real-world phenomena. This skill is crucial, as it extends beyond solving classroom problems to include identifying ambiguous real-world issues and structuring them into clear, solvable mathematical models.

Foundational research by mathematics educator Alan H. Schoenfeld (1985) first established the importance of problem-solving tasks in developing deeper mathematical understanding, and research continues to strongly reinforce this. Meta-analyses by Kong and colleagues (2021) demonstrate that effective problem-solving instruction significantly improves students' ability to transfer mathematical knowledge to novel situations. This finding is further supported by Sara Cothren Cook, Lauren W. Collins, Lisa L. Morin, and Paul J. Riccomini (2020), whose research shows that schema-based instruction in mathematical problem solving enhances students' capacity to tackle complex, real-world mathematical challenges. Additionally, Corey Peltier and Kimberly J. Vannest's (2017) meta-analysis confirms that systematic instruction in problem-solving strategies leads to improved mathematical outcomes across diverse student populations.

While students typically encounter well-defined problems in educational settings, the real world often presents complex situations where the problem is not explicitly given. Effective problem solving equips students to navigate these scenarios by formulating relevant mathematical questions and developing models that provide insights into answering them. For example, students might engage in a project to model the environmental impact of their school. They could collect data on the school's energy consumption, waste production, and water usage. From here, they could develop mathematical models to predict how changes in school policies or student behavior could reduce the school's carbon footprint. Such a task would involve the following.

- **Statistical analysis:** Gathering and analyzing data to understand current consumption and waste patterns
- **Algebraic modeling:** Creating formulas that predict outcomes based on various hypothetical changes
- **Interpretation and decision making:** Using the model to propose and evaluate the effectiveness of different conservation strategies

This type of modeling activity helps students apply their mathematical skills in meaningful contexts and enhance their understanding of the impact of environmental policies. It promotes a holistic understanding of how mathematical thinking can address and inform real-world issues. Moreover, problem solving requires familiarity with a variety of solution strategies and the judgment to select the most appropriate one for a specific problem. Developing this competence involves extensive practice with diverse problems across various contexts, which not only reinforces mathematical skills but also fosters adaptability and innovation in thinking.

Another illustrative example could involve modeling traffic flow around the school to improve safety and efficiency. Students might analyze traffic patterns at key times during the school day and use geometric or algebraic models to simulate various traffic management strategies, such as changes in signal timing or the introduction of new routes for buses and cars. This project could include the following.

- **Geometric reasoning:** Mapping out the school area and identifying critical points for traffic congestion
- **Differential equations:** Modeling traffic flow using equations that describe the rate of change in car density at different times and locations
- **Optimization:** Applying mathematical strategies to find the best solutions for reducing congestion and increasing safety

By integrating these components of problem solving and modeling into the curriculum, educators can cultivate an environment that encourages students to see mathematics as a practical and powerful tool for making sense of complex problems. This perspective not only prepares students for academic success but also equips them for thoughtful, analytical, and proactive engagement with the challenges of the world they live in.

In the following pages, we'll further explore the essence of problem solving and modeling, the cultivation of inventive problem-solving skills, the development of effective modeling techniques, the interplay between this competency and that of the previous chapter, and strategies to enhance problem solving and modeling.

The Essence of Problem Solving and Modeling

In the CMC framework, developing problem-solving and modeling skills begins with effectively representing problems mathematically using various methods, such as numerically, symbolically, verbally, or graphically. This skill extends beyond simply recognizing numbers; it requires comprehensive understanding and visualization of the problem's key elements, focusing on essential relationships and omitting nonessential information.

Research underlines the importance of such contextual and engaging approaches to teaching mathematics. According to findings from education professors and researchers Douglas H. Clements and Julie Sarama (2021), engaging students with practical, visually supported mathematics problems that relate closely to their experiences significantly enhances their understanding of mathematical concepts and boosts their problem-solving skills. These approaches not only make learning mathematics more interesting and relevant but also help students develop a stronger, more durable understanding of key mathematical operations and reasoning skills. By focusing on context-rich, engaging mathematical activities tailored to appropriate developmental stages, educators can effectively promote deeper mathematical comprehension and critical thinking from an early age.

For instance, consider a typical problem faced by third graders who might need to figure out the total number of apples collected from two trees if one tree has double the apples of another. Instead of immediately seizing on the numbers and calculating, the students receive encouragement from their teacher to develop a more strategic understanding. They might start by drawing a simple diagram representing the two trees, labeling one tree with a specific number of apples and the other with double that amount. This visual representation helps solidify their understanding of the problem's structure—focusing on the relationship between the numbers rather than the numbers themselves.

Accurately representing a problem often requires building a mental image of its essential components. This process steers students away from *number grabbing*—a common but less effective strategy where students hastily pick numbers to perform operations. Instead, teachers guide students toward methods that foster the development of problem models. These models involve constructing a mental or tangible representation that maintains the structural relations among the variables described in the problem.

To illustrate, let's consider a basic arithmetic problem that might appear in an elementary classroom: A baker used 250 grams of flour to make a small batch of cookies and three times as much for a large batch. How much flour did the baker use in total?

In a superficial approach, students might focus merely on the numbers—250 grams and three times—and quickly perform multiplication followed by addition. However, a more proficient approach would include visualizing the problem with a bar model or a simple equation. Students could represent the small batch with a bar representing 250 grams and the large batch with a larger bar of three equal segments, each representing that number. They would then sum these to find the total amount of flour used.

This modeling approach encourages students to think about the relationships between quantities and operations, and thereby foster a deeper understanding of the mathematical concepts involved. It helps them distinguish between known and unknown quantities and focus their attention on how these quantities interact within the problem context.

Moreover, successful problem solvers often engage more with the relational aspects of a problem than with its mere numerical details. For instance, they might consider the significance of the phrase *three times as much* not just as a cue for multiplication but as a relational indicator between two quantities. Less successful solvers tend to fixate on individual numbers and operational keywords without grasping these deeper connections.

In summary, the development of problem solving and modeling within the mathematics classroom comprises moving students from superficial engagement with numbers to more profound interaction with the mathematical relationships that those numbers represent. This shift enhances their ability to solve individual problems and also builds a foundational understanding that supports more complex mathematical thinking in later grades. To become proficient in problem solving, students must learn to effectively recognize and represent mathematical situations. This includes seeing beyond the superficial details of a problem to the underlying mathematical structures that various problems may share. Beginner problem solvers often focus on the immediate, visible aspects of a scenario—like specific characters or settings—while more advanced solvers discern the fundamental mathematical relationships that guide how the problem should be approached and solved.

For example, consider a problem asking students to figure out how many different outfits can be created using five specific pieces of clothing—each piece either worn or not worn. Another problem could include calculating the number of different outcomes possible when flipping a coin five times. Although the contexts are vastly different—one being about fashion choices and the other about probability—the mathematical challenge is the same. Each problem involves making five binary (yes/no, on/off) decisions. By understanding such similarities, students can apply the same mathematical strategies—such as using powers of two for binary decisions—to a wide range of problems. This capability to abstract common mathematical structures from diverse situations is a hallmark of advanced problem-solving skills. This skill set progresses as students learn to create accurate mental models of problems, highlighting key mathematical relationships and excluding irrelevant details. For example, when solving a problem related to the possible combinations of pizza toppings (choosing *yes* or *no* for each topping, like mushrooms, peppers, and onions), students should focus on the combinations rather than the toppings themselves.

Flexibility in problem solving—an essential trait for proficiency—develops as students encounter a broad spectrum of problems. This variety encourages them to adapt known strategies to new situations, and it enhances their ability to handle both routine tasks and novel challenges. For instance, understanding binary decision making in the contexts of clothing, coin flips, and pizza toppings prepares students to apply this strategy to any situation involving binary choices, even unfamiliar scenarios. Cultivating this flexibility requires presenting students with problems that might look different on the surface but share deep structural similarities. This practice helps them recognize and exploit these commonalities, thereby broadening their mathematical understanding and improving their ability to apply learned concepts across various contexts. As a result, students become adept at solving a wide range of mathematical problems and also grow in their capacity to think critically and adaptively, which prepares them for complex problem solving beyond the classroom.

The Cultivation of Inventive Problem-Solving Skills

The CMC framework promotes inventive problem solving by encouraging students to think outside the box and come up with multiple solutions to a given problem. This not only fosters creativity but also builds resilience, as students learn that there can be many paths to the right answer and that arriving at a solution may require persistence and flexibility. These skills are invaluable in a rapidly changing world where new problems and technologies constantly emerge, requiring novel approaches and solutions. In that context, the following sections will cover mathematical problem types along with flexible thinking.

Mathematical Problem Types

Educators differentiate between two main types of mathematical challenges: (1) routine problems and (2) nonroutine problems. Mastery of both is crucial for developing problem-solving skills that are versatile and applicable in real-world settings. *Routine problems* are characterized by their straightforward nature, where the solution method is already known to the learner. Solving these problems takes *reproductive thinking*, where the learner simply needs to recall and apply an established procedure. For example, a typical routine problem could involve multiplying two-digit numbers, such as 34×12. Most adults and many school-age children know the multiplication algorithm needed to solve this, making it a routine problem. In contrast, *nonroutine problems* are those for which no solution method is immediately apparent. These problems demand what is known as *productive thinking*, where the learner must creatively devise a strategy to understand and solve the problem. Consider the following scenario.

Problem statement: A classroom has 18 students, and the teacher wants to arrange their desks in equal rows and equal columns without any desks leftover. How should the desks be arranged?

- *Visual representation*—One way to approach this problem is to experiment with different configurations. A student might try to draw the arrangement on paper, testing various layouts, like 2 rows of 9 and 3 rows of 6. This method allows them to visually verify which setup utilizes all desks while maintaining equal rows and columns.

- *Systematic trial and error*—Alternatively, students might engage in a systematic trial-and-error process. They could list all factors of 18 and test each pair to see which can form a complete rectangle, ultimately determining that 3 rows of 6 desks each fits the criteria.

- *Algebraic method*—A more mathematical approach involves recognizing the problem as one of finding factors of a number. By identifying that 18 can be factored into 1 and 18, 2 and 9, or 3 and 6, students can conclude that several configurations are possible, such as 3 rows of 6 desks.

- *Problem-solving skills*—A student skilled in problem solving would be able to identify these different methods and choose the most effective one based on the circumstances. This skill requires a flexibility in thinking and a capacity to adapt approaches based on the problem context, whether it requires a simple calculation, a visual layout, or an algebraic solution.

Cultivating problem-solving abilities involves exposing students to a wide variety of problems and encouraging them to think about different ways to approach them. This helps them develop their mathematical skills and apply these skills in practical, often unfamiliar situations. Developing a deep understanding of how to navigate both routine and nonroutine problems prepares students for complex problem solving in the real world, where challenges rarely come with a predefined method of solution.

Flexible Thinking

Flexibility in problem-solving approaches is crucial, especially when tackling nonroutine problems that require adaptive and innovative thinking. This flexibility often manifests in the ability to devise or modify methods according to the unique demands of unfamiliar situations. A key aspect of this skill is the use of general mathematical principles, such as proportions, to make informed decisions in everyday scenarios.

Consider a situation where a family is trying to determine the most cost-effective way to buy fruit juice for a week. They encounter several options: a 1-liter bottle priced at $3, a 1.5-liter bottle for $4, and a 2-liter bottle for $5. To decide which offers the best value for money, they can employ different strategies.

- **Ratio strategy:** Analyzing the cost relative to the quantity, they might calculate the price per liter for each option. The 1-liter bottle costs $3 per liter, the 1.5-liter bottle approximately $2.67 per liter, and the 2-liter bottle $2.50 per liter. This straightforward proportional comparison shows that the 2-liter bottle offers the most juice for the least money, identifying it as the best buy.

- **Total cost modeling:** If the family knows their weekly juice consumption is about 6 liters, they could model the total cost for each option. Six 1-liter bottles cost $18, four 1.5-liter bottles cost $16, and three 2-liter bottles cost only $15. This model illustrates that, for the family's specific needs, purchasing 2-liter bottles is the most economical over a week.

- **Break-even analysis:** In a scenario where budget constraints are tighter, the family might need to consider how soon they would "break even" with each purchase. For example, if buying in larger quantities means saving more in the long run but spending more up front, they could calculate the point at which the larger upfront cost balances out against the ongoing savings.

In another context, imagine a teacher setting up a classroom and choosing between different packs of markers. One option features 30 markers for $15, and another offers 50 markers for $20. Here, the problem solving includes the following.

- **Unit cost calculation:** Calculating the cost per marker would reveal that the first pack costs 50 cents per marker, while the second costs 40 cents per marker. Thus, the second pack provides better value.

- **Usage and demand modeling:** If the markers are known to dry out quickly, the teacher might model the expected lifespan of each pack based on daily usage rates and decide whether the lower cost per marker justifies buying the larger pack, considering the potential for waste.

These examples showcase how problem solving in nonroutine scenarios greatly benefits from a flexible approach that allows individuals to tailor their strategies to specific circumstances and available data. This not only aids practical decision making but also enhances understanding of broader mathematical concepts like ratios, unit costs, and proportional reasoning. When problem solving is integrated into the decision-making process, students and adults alike can improve their cognitive flexibility and practical application of mathematical concepts, as well as develop a deeper appreciation for the utility of mathematics in navigating real-world situations.

The Development of Effective Modeling Techniques

Effective modeling techniques are crucial in developing problem-solving skills because they allow students to represent real-world scenarios through mathematical frameworks. Modeling is particularly important as students start to understand the applications of mathematics in everyday life, which ultimately prepares them for advanced studies and data-driven fields such as engineering and economics. Teachers might employ the following types of modeling techniques.

- **Graphical models:** Young students might begin by using simple line graphs to track daily temperature changes and help them visualize and understand weather patterns. In a middle school setting, students could use bar graphs to compare the total books read by students in different classes, thus making data comparison accessible and engaging.

- **Algebraic models:** At the middle school level, students might learn to express relationships using simple algebraic equations. For example, if a car travels at a constant speed, students could model the relationship between distance and time with the equation $d = rt$, where d is distance, r is rate, and t is time. This helps them predict how far the car will travel in a given time at a specified speed.

- **Statistical models:** Elementary students might predict the outcome of tossing coins or rolling dice and compare their predictions to actual results, introducing basic probability concepts. Middle school students might use more sophisticated statistical models to analyze the results of school surveys, such as questions about students' favorite lunch foods or sports, and learn to calculate averages and mode.

- **Simulation models:** In middle school science, students could use simulations to model ecosystems. For example, they might predict what would happen to a pond ecosystem if the number of fish increased or decreased, learning about the balance of ecosystems and the impact of changes within them.

- **Optimization models:** A practical example to introduce younger students to basic concepts of optimization and efficiency could involve arranging classroom desks to maximize available space or planning the shortest route for a school field trip.

Teaching students to think about how mathematics can explain and influence the world requires them to actively engage with real data and scenarios. Activities should encourage them to collect data, create models, test these models, and refine their approaches based on observations and outcomes. Such educational experiences enhance mathematical skills and also promote analytical thinking.

Incorporating technology can make these activities more engaging. For instance, using tablets or computers to create interactive graphs or simulate ecological changes can make the learning process more dynamic and accessible, allowing students to explore complex concepts in a user-friendly environment. By weaving in these modeling techniques, you equip students with a comprehensive set of problem-solving tools essential for their academic success and future professional endeavors. As students grow more proficient with these techniques, they're better prepared to tackle more complex problems and make meaningful contributions in various fields.

Interplay Among Problem Solving, Modeling, Procedural Fluency, and Conceptual Understanding

The competencies in the CMC framework are designed to work in harmony to foster holistic mathematical proficiency. While all the competencies are interconnected, the interplay between problem solving and modeling and conceptual and procedural integration (chapter 2, page 25) is particularly pronounced. This section highlights the dynamic relationship of these competencies, emphasizing how strong problem-solving skills and effective modeling are enhanced by procedural fluency and deep conceptual understanding, and vice versa. This interplay is essential for developing a nuanced understanding of mathematics, making it critical to explore in greater detail.

Problem solving, modeling, conceptual understanding, and procedural fluency are mutually supportive of one another, as demonstrated by various approaches to typical mathematical challenges. Developing methods of solving nonroutine problems relies not just on an understanding of the quantities involved and their relationships but on fluency in addressing routine problems. Similarly, the skill in addressing nonroutine challenges provides context and motivation for mastering routine problems and for grasping concepts such as variables, conditions, and solutions.

Consider a classroom scenario where students are learning to solve word problems involving addition and subtraction. A nonroutine problem might include determining how many apples are left in a basket after some have been given away, based on a story narrative. To solve this, students must understand the quantities involved (total apples, apples given away), their relationship, and how to represent this situation mathematically.

In this context, problem solving and modeling come into play as the students learn how to perform operations like two-digit addition and subtraction. For example, students might initially use a physical model, such as counting blocks or drawing tally marks, to understand and solve a problem like $78 + 24$. They might visually represent the two numbers with groups of blocks or marks, then physically combine them to see the resulting quantity. As students progress, they transition from these conceptually transparent but effortful methods to more streamlined and efficient ones. A more clipped procedure would involve teaching them the standard numerical algorithm for addition, where they learn to carry over numbers without the need for physical counting aids. This progression illustrates how students use problem solving and modeling to navigate from a basic understanding of a concept toward procedural fluency. This evolution in learning methods not only enhances their ability to tackle straightforward mathematical problems but also supports their engagement with more complex challenges. For example, when students use models to solve subtraction problems such as $86 - 53$, they begin with a concrete representation, perhaps using a base-ten blocks model. They would start with 8 ten blocks and 6 one blocks, then decompose one of the ten blocks to make up the difference needed for subtraction, visually and physically manipulating the blocks to find the solution.

As they develop their mathematical thinking, students learn to effectively select among different procedures. They also discover that successful problem solving depends on the ability to readily perform operations. Moreover, engaging with challenging problems enhances their capacity to acquire new mathematical concepts and skills. This adaptive reasoning, which young learners often naturally exhibit, shows early signs of strategic thinking as students choose strategies suited to specific problems. This dynamic interplay of modeling, problem solving, and procedural fluency is fundamental in equipping students with the skills necessary to navigate both academic challenges and practical situations. It fosters a robust mathematical foundation that empowers students to approach complex problems with confidence and creativity.

Strategies to Enhance Problem Solving and Modeling

To effectively develop your students' problem-solving and modeling skills, consider implementing the following strategies: multiple solutions, real-life scenarios, collaborative problem solving, and process over the product.

Encourage Exploration of Multiple Solutions

Challenging students to find different solutions to a single problem deepens their understanding of mathematical concepts, fosters flexible thinking, and strengthens problem-solving skills. Encouraging multiple methods helps students see that mathematics is not just about memorizing formulas but about thinking creatively and making connections between different strategies.

Example: Calculating the area of a room

Consider a practical example—a renovation project where students are asked to calculate the area of a room. Instead of directing them to use one specific formula, encourage students to explore various methods for arriving at the solution.

- *Decomposition into simpler shapes*—Students could divide the room into smaller, manageable sections, such as rectangles, triangles, or other shapes they recognize. By breaking the problem into parts, students can apply familiar area formulas and sum the results, reinforcing their understanding of how complex shapes can be simplified.

- *Direct application of formulas*—If the room has a standard shape, such as a rectangle, students can directly apply the area formula. This reinforces the procedural skill of applying the correct formula for a given shape but allows flexibility if students encounter a space that is not a perfect rectangle.

- *Estimation using known measurements*—When the room is irregularly shaped or precision isn't critical, students could use estimation strategies based on known measurements. They might estimate the room's dimensions using measuring tools or previously known facts about standard measurements, promoting real-world applicability and flexible reasoning.

This approach helps students appreciate the flexibility of mathematical thinking, showing them that there are often multiple pathways to a solution. It also builds their confidence in tackling real-world problems because they know they have a tool kit of strategies they can apply depending on the situation. Furthermore, it encourages reflection—students can compare the results of different methods and discuss which approach might be most efficient, accurate, or appropriate for a particular problem. This process of comparison helps them internalize the strengths and limitations of various mathematical strategies.

Use Real-Life Scenarios

Incorporating real-life scenarios into mathematics instruction helps bridge the gap between abstract concepts and their practical applications. When students work on problems that reflect situations they may encounter in their daily lives or future careers, they see the relevance of what they are learning and gain valuable skills that are useful beyond the classroom. This relevance not only increases student engagement but also fosters a deeper understanding of how mathematical skills are applicable in a wide range of contexts.

Example 1: Budgeting for a school carnival

A practical problem could involve designing a budget for a school event. Students would need to calculate costs for food, decorations, venue rental, and other event-related expenses. This task encourages them to apply mathematical concepts like addition, subtraction, multiplication, and percentages in a real-world context. They would also need to make decisions about allocating limited resources, introducing an element of financial literacy.

Objective: Students will apply mathematical concepts to plan and budget a school carnival, fostering problem-solving and financial literacy skills.

Materials needed:

- Calculators
- Spreadsheet software (such as Microsoft Excel or Google Sheets)
- Price lists for food supplies, games, and rental equipment

Instructions:

1. *Outline of the carnival*—Start by defining the scope of the carnival, including various categories such as food, games, attractions, and prizes.
2. *Group assignment*—Divide the class into small groups, with each group taking responsibility for a different aspect of the carnival, such as food, games, or decorations.
3. *Budget calculation*—Each group calculates the total expected costs, considering different suppliers and varying quantities. They should consider the price per item and the total items required.
4. *Algebraic application*—Encourage students to use algebraic equations to adjust quantities and costs to ensure they remain within a predetermined budget. This might involve setting up equations to solve for unknown quantities or adjusting variables to meet financial constraints.

Problem Solving and Modeling   63

5. *Presentation and review*—Each group presents their budgeting decisions and the mathematical strategies they employed. This step allows students to articulate their thought process and receive feedback on their approach.

The following corresponding mathematical challenges cover different instructional levels, beginning with elementary school.

Problem: Calculate the total number of bottled drinks needed if each attendee is expected to purchase 1 drink, and each drink costs $1.50. Assume there are 200 attendees.

Mathematical content: Basic multiplication and addition

Modeling: Students might use physical counters or draw diagrams to visualize the quantity of drinks against the total attendees.

Pedagogy: This introduces young students to simple budgeting and the concept of unit cost, embedding foundational arithmetic skills in a real-world context.

A middle school example is as follows.

Problem: Consider the scenario for pizza (200 attendees, 50% likely to buy pizza, $10 per pizza, 8 slices per pizza).

Mathematical content: Fractions, percentages, and multiplication

Modeling: Students create a spreadsheet model to calculate different scenarios (for example, 40%, 50%, and 60% of attendees buying pizza) and find the most cost-effective option.

Pedagogy: This reinforces concepts of fractions and percentages and encourages students to explore the impact of different assumptions on their budget, thus enhancing their analytical skills.

Finally, here is a high school example.

Problem: Optimize the total cost by choosing between different suppliers offering volume discounts for bulk purchases of prizes for games.

> **Mathematical content:** Algebraic equations, systems of inequalities, and possibly elements of calculus if optimizing within constraints
>
> **Modeling:** Students might develop a mathematical model using algebraic expressions to represent cost per unit, and apply constraints to determine the minimum cost.
>
> **Pedagogy:** This introduces more complex mathematical concepts such as systems of equations and inequalities and provides students with a practical application of algebra and optimization.

These examples not only illustrate the application of mathematical concepts across various instructional levels but also highlight the importance of problem solving and modeling in making informed decisions. Through such activities, students learn to apply mathematical reasoning to solve practical problems, preparing them for real-life challenges beyond the classroom.

> **Example 2:** Calculating environmental impact
>
> Another scenario could involve calculating the environmental impact of everyday behaviors. For instance, you could ask students to estimate how much water a household uses in a week and how that usage could be reduced by implementing conservation strategies. They could then calculate the environmental and financial savings over time. This introduces mathematical skills such as multiplication, division, and unit conversion, while also raising awareness about sustainability.

Through this type of problem solving, students practice mathematics and engage with real-world issues, and thereby see how their decisions can affect the environment. This makes learning more meaningful and inspires them to think critically about the world around them.

When their tasks use real-life scenarios, students are more likely to stay engaged with the material because they can see the practical relevance of the mathematical skills they are developing. Moreover, these tasks allow students to practice critical thinking and problem solving in contexts that mimic situations they may face outside of school. The ability to apply mathematical concepts to everyday life helps build their confidence and prepares them for future challenges, both personal and professional.

Promote Collaborative Problem Solving

Encouraging students to work together on complex problems creates a dynamic learning environment where ideas can be exchanged and understanding deepened. Collaborative problem solving helps students approach tasks from multiple perspectives, which fosters mathematical and scientific skills as well as essential teamwork and communication skills. Working in groups allows students to learn from one another and build their confidence as they contribute unique strengths to solving a problem.

An example collaborative problem-solving task is a project focused on modeling the effects of pollution on a local ecosystem. In this scenario, students are divided into teams, with each team responsible for analyzing a different variable affecting the ecosystem.

Example: Modeling the effects of pollution on a local ecosystem

- *Team 1: Water quality*—This team might examine how pollutants in the water affect plant and animal life, using mathematical models to track changes over time.

- *Team 2: Wildlife impact*—Another team could focus on how pollution affects local wildlife, using data to predict population declines or changes in migration patterns.

- *Team 3: Pollution sources*—A third team could investigate where pollution is coming from (factories, agriculture, and so on), modeling how different sources contribute to overall ecosystem damage.

By handling different variables and working together to understand the whole system, students develop specific mathematical and scientific skills (such as data analysis, modeling, and statistics) as well as practice collaboration and communication. At the end of the project, all teams present their findings and combine them to form a comprehensive picture of the ecosystem's health.

Collaborative problem solving allows students to engage in peer learning, where they can explain concepts to one another, fill gaps in each other's understanding, and approach problems from different angles. This type of environment mirrors the real world, where teamwork is often essential to solving complex problems in fields like engineering, science, and business.

Additionally, working together helps students develop soft skills like communication, conflict resolution, and leadership, which are critical in both academic and professional settings. It also builds their confidence in their own abilities as they meaningfully contribute to a group effort.

Collaborative problem solving enhances student engagement, as learners feel accountable for not only their own understanding but the group's success. They are motivated to actively participate, knowing that their contributions impact the outcome of the entire project.

Focus on the Process Over the Product

In mathematics, it is easy for students to become fixated on getting the right answer, but true understanding comes from the journey taken to reach that solution. Emphasizing the importance of the problem-solving process encourages students to value their reasoning and the steps they take, rather than simply focusing on whether they arrive at the correct answer. This shift in focus fosters critical thinking, metacognitive skills, and a more thoughtful approach to problem solving. The following are strategies for focusing on the process.

- **Thought process documentation:** Encourage students to keep track of their thinking as they work through problems. They could do this through journal entries where they document the strategies they considered, the decisions they made, and the challenges they faced along the way. Reflecting on their own process allows them to see what worked, what didn't, and why.

For example, in solving a complex algebraic equation, students might record how they tried to simplify the expression, what strategies they used to eliminate variables, and how they overcame any mistakes. This process of documentation helps students recognize patterns in their problem-solving approach and learn from their experience.

- **Group discussions and reflection:** After students complete a problem, facilitate group discussions where they share the strategies they used. This allows them to see multiple methods of approaching the same problem and opens up conversations about why certain methods might be more efficient or intuitive. By reflecting on their own work and considering alternatives, students begin to appreciate the various ways a problem can be solved.

For instance, after a geometry problem on calculating the area of an irregular shape, students could discuss whether decomposing the shape into known figures was more effective than using a grid approximation. This conversation reinforces the idea that there isn't always a single "right" approach, and each method has its strengths.

Example: Reflection in problem solving

One way to implement this focus on process could be to have students solve a challenging problem and then write a reflection on their approach. For instance, after completing a problem about optimizing the cost of materials for building a structure, students might reflect on the decisions they made regarding material choices, the constraints they faced, and the mathematical techniques they applied.

Did they use algebra to minimize cost? Did they struggle with certain parts of the problem, and if so, how did they overcome those struggles? These reflections can help students internalize the lessons learned, even if they didn't arrive at the correct final answer.

By focusing on the process, students develop a deeper understanding of mathematical concepts because they learn not just what to do but why they are doing it. This approach helps students do the following.

- **Develop metacognition:** Students become more aware of their own thinking and learning processes, which is essential for long-term success.

- **Build resilience:** By valuing the process, students become less discouraged by mistakes and more motivated to persevere through difficult problems.

- **Gain flexibility:** When students document and discuss their approaches, they become more open to alternative methods and strategies, building flexibility in their thinking. Shifting the focus from product to process also helps students approach mathematics with a growth mindset, recognizing that the most important learning often happens during the struggle to find a solution, not necessarily in the solution itself.

- **Integrate technology and tools:** Utilize technological tools to enhance the modeling aspects of problem solving. Applications that simulate physical processes or allow for dynamic statistical analysis can provide hands-on experiences in creating and manipulating mathematical models. For instance, graphing calculators or software like Desmos can help with visualizing mathematical relationships and exploring the effects of changing variables in real time. This integration aids students in understanding complex concepts and also engages them in interactive learning experiences. More detailed exploration of the strategic use of tools and technology appears in chapter 6 (page 121).

By integrating these strategies into your teaching practices, you can significantly enhance your students' ability to tackle mathematical challenges. This not only prepares them for academic success but also equips them with the analytical skills necessary for thoughtful and effective problem solving in various contexts.

Conclusion

In this chapter on problem solving and modeling within the CMC framework, we've explored how dynamic, application-oriented approaches to mathematics education can profoundly enrich students' learning experiences. By moving away from traditional, rote memorization methods and embracing real-world problems that require a deep understanding of mathematical concepts and a keen ability to model various scenarios, we help students learn mathematics and apply it innovatively and effectively in their lives.

The activities and strategies outlined in this chapter serve as crucial building blocks for cultivating strong problem-solving and modeling skills. These exercises are not just about finding the right answers; they are about exploring, experimenting, and understanding the processes that lead to those answers. Through the lens of the CMC framework, these problem-solving and modeling tasks do more than teach mathematics—they prepare students for the future. They equip learners to think critically and creatively, to tackle complex problems with confidence, and to approach challenges with a robust tool kit of mathematical strategies. This preparation is essential, as the problems our students will face in the real world will often lack clear instructions or a single correct answer. Furthermore, the integration of real-life scenarios helps students see the relevance of mathematics in everyday life, enhancing their motivation and engagement. By collaboratively working on these problems, students also develop key social skills such as communication, teamwork, and respect for diverse perspectives, which are just as important as the mathematical concepts themselves.

As this chapter concludes, it is clear that the art of problem solving and modeling is central to developing comprehensive mathematical proficiency. These skills are vital not just in academic settings but amid the complex realities of our world. The strategic use of tools and technologies, as discussed in chapter 6 (page 121), further amplifies this competency, enabling students to perform sophisticated analyses and make informed decisions based on sound mathematical reasoning.

Thus, the journey through problem solving and modeling is more than just an academic exercise; it is a fundamental part of shaping thoughtful, capable individuals who can apply their knowledge to make a positive impact in their communities and beyond. As educators, we must continue nurturing these skills with intention and insight to ensure that all students have the opportunity to thrive in an increasingly mathematical world.

CHAPTER 4

Logical Reasoning and Proof

Logical reasoning forms the bedrock of effective mathematical understanding; it allows students to methodically explore relationships between concepts and real-world applications. This skill is crucial for constructing arguments that are both sound and convincingly justified, relying on thorough examination of various possibilities. Logical reasoning acts as the connective tissue that links diverse mathematical elements—such as facts, procedures, and theories—into an integrated, sensible whole.

In the context of mathematics education, logical reasoning plays a pivotal role in the development and understanding of mathematical proofs. Proof, a fundamental element of mathematics, involves confirming the truth of a statement through systematic, logical deduction from agreed-on premises. This deductive reasoning is what sets mathematical proof apart from less structured forms of reasoning, imbuing it with clarity and precision.

Consider a classic example used in geometry classes: proving that the sum of the interior angles of any triangle is 180 degrees. This proof typically begins with known principles, and through a sequence of logical deductions—perhaps involving drawing an auxiliary line or considering the alternate angles theorem—leads to the desired conclusion. This process not only demonstrates the power of logical reasoning but also highlights the necessity of a structured approach in mathematics.

Logical reasoning also empowers students to independently resolve mathematical disputes. In mathematics, the validity of a solution is determined through transparent logical processes, not opinion or authority. When disagreements arise, students can trace back through their steps to ensure that each part of their reasoning logically follows from what preceded it. This practice both builds their confidence in mathematics and enhances their problem-solving skills by reinforcing the importance of a logical foundation.

Furthermore, the skills developed through logical reasoning extend beyond academic applications. They are crucial in everyday decision making and problem solving. For example, when students plan projects or organize tasks, they often use logical sequencing to determine the most efficient order of operations. Whether they are programming a robot in a technology class or planning a fundraising event, the ability to reason logically ensures that their projects are well organized and effectively executed.

Incorporating logical reasoning and proof into mathematics education involves more than just teaching students to solve equations or complete geometric proofs; it means engaging them with puzzles that challenge their deductive skills, presenting scenarios that require careful analysis, or integrating real-life problems that necessitate systematic planning and reasoning.

This chapter delves into effective teaching strategies for fostering logical reasoning, examines detailed examples of how logical reasoning can be applied in classroom settings, and discusses the significant role that logical reasoning plays in helping students navigate their academic and everyday lives. By prioritizing this competency, educators enhance students' mathematical proficiency and equip them with the critical thinking capabilities necessary to tackle complex challenges across various domains.

The Essence of Logical Reasoning and Proof

An essential component of logical reasoning in mathematics is the skill to justify one's mathematical approaches and solutions. The term *justify* here refers to providing a robust rationale for the decisions made during problem solving. Although proofs represent the most structured form of justification, requiring rigorous logical completeness, everyday justifications in a classroom setting might be more succinct, aiming to sketch out the underlying logic rather than elaborate every detail.

Understanding justification and proof is crucial in mathematics and often viewed as a domain for advanced students. However, the foundational skills necessary for this complex task begin to develop much earlier, right from the elementary levels of education. Encouraging learners to start justifying their mathematical thinking from an early age sets a precedent for deeper engagement with mathematics as they progress through their education. In practical terms, educators can initiate this process in the early grades by integrating justification into regular classroom activities. For example, when students in kindergarten or first grade solve problems involving basic addition or subtraction, teachers can prompt them to explain why they chose a particular method or approach. Students could describe why they decided to use physical counters to solve an addition problem, explaining how this method helps them visualize the numbers and better understand the concept of addition.

Establishing a classroom norm where justification of mathematical ideas is routinely expected can profoundly impact students' ability to articulate and refine their thinking. This practice encourages students to not only provide reasons for their immediate choices but also connect their reasoning to broader mathematical principles. For instance, when students discuss how grouping objects helps them count faster, they are not just justifying their current method—they are laying the groundwork for understanding multiplication as repeated addition.

You can facilitate this by creating an environment where students feel comfortable voicing their thoughts and are encouraged to think critically about their own and others' mathematical reasoning. Group discussions, peer reviews, and presentations in which you task students with explaining their solutions to the class are all ways to help achieve such as environment. Such activities enhance individual understanding as well as build a collaborative learning atmosphere that values clear communication and logical reasoning. By nurturing these skills from the beginning of learners' education, teachers help students develop a clear, logical approach to problem solving that goes beyond mere calculation. This prepares them for higher-level mathematics, which heavily relies on proofs and justifications, and also for real-world situations where logical reasoning is key to making informed decisions.

The Development and Application of Logical Reasoning and Proof

Research by Stephanie M. Carlson (2005) demonstrates that students as young as four and five years old exhibit sophisticated cognitive skills when solving mathematical problems, including the ability to use executive function for reasoning and making logical inferences. These findings are reinforced by research from Robin Jacob and Julia Parkinson (2015), which shows that young children's capacity for logical reasoning is closely tied to their academic achievement in mathematics. Furthermore, Paul L. Morgan, George Farkas, and Steve Maczuga (2015) document how early elementary students display remarkable resilience to incorrect suggestions when solving mathematical problems, an early indication of critical thinking and mathematical reasoning capabilities. These capabilities can be further developed through carefully designed activities that enhance students' ability to construct and understand representations.

For example, in an elementary school setting, first graders might be introduced to concepts of mathematical proof through simple grouping and number-partitioning activities. A teacher might set up an exercise where students must determine whether the number of objects grouped in twos and threes always results in even or odd sums. By manipulating physical objects such as beads or blocks, learners can visually and tactilely verify their findings, thereby engaging in foundational proof-like reasoning.

By third grade, students are ready to explore more complex operations, such as the basics of multiplication and division, with real-world applications. You could create an activity where students need to calculate how many plates can be set on some tables if each table can hold four plates and there are six tables. This scenario helps students apply multiplication in a context that makes sense to them, grounding abstract concepts in tangible reality.

Moving into upper elementary, fourth graders can handle even more sophisticated mathematical challenges that require logical deductions. For instance, you could task students with figuring out how many pages they can print if they have three ink cartridges and each cartridge allows for three hundred pages to be printed. This problem introduces them to the concept of multiplication for larger numbers and provides a practical application that they can visualize and logically reason through.

Logical reasoning begins with the ability to connect and sequence ideas. For students, this means learning to follow a line of reasoning from premises to a conclusion. A practical approach to developing this skill in the classroom involves the use of conditional statements and logical connectives. For instance, a middle school teacher might introduce a geometry lesson by asking students to consider the statement, "If a figure is a square, then it has four right angles." Students can then examine various figures and apply this conditional logic to determine whether each figure qualifies as a square based on its properties. This activity helps students understand geometric concepts, and it also trains them in the process of logical deduction.

Students also apply logical reasoning to solve mathematical problems where they must decide the best approach. For example, when faced with complex algebraic equations, students should first identify what is known and what needs to be found, and then choose an appropriate method to solve the equations. This might require isolating variables, manipulating equations, or setting up systems of equations based on the relationships defined in the problems. In a classroom setting, you can enhance these skills by engaging students in problem-solving activities that require them to justify their methods and solutions. A practical exercise could involve breaking students into groups to solve different types of equations and then present their solutions and reasoning to the class. This helps them understand the subject matter and also practice communicating mathematical ideas clearly and effectively.

The introduction of proofs in mathematics education serves as an advanced application of logical reasoning. Teaching students to construct proofs involves guiding them to use axioms, definitions, and previously established theorems to build arguments that confirm the truth of new theorems. Starting with simple proofs in geometry, such as proving the properties of parallel lines or the Pythagorean theorem, can be an effective way to introduce this concept. For students in grades K–2, proofs might begin with simpler, more intuitive exercises. For example, using visual aids, you might demonstrate that the angles in a triangle always add up to 180 degrees by cutting out the angles and arranging them in a straight line. As students progress, they can move to more formal proofs, using algebraic identities or logical statements to demonstrate their understanding of mathematical properties.

Interplay Between Logical Reasoning and Other Competencies

Logical reasoning is pivotal in how it interacts with other core competencies within the CMC framework, especially during problem-solving activities. As learners tackle mathematical challenges, they deploy a combination of their competencies in a fluid and integrative manner to effectively navigate problems.

- **Problem solving and problem formulation:** Initially, learners utilize their problem-solving skills to formulate and represent problems. This might involve heuristic methods that suggest potential solutions or strategies. For instance, when they encounter a complex algebraic problem, students might first identify patterns or use simpler numbers to test their ideas before they apply these strategies to more complex numbers.

- **Conceptual understanding:** Conceptual understanding provides essential background knowledge and mental models that support logical reasoning. As students work through a problem, they may employ various mathematical concepts or visual representations to aid their reasoning. For example, in tackling fraction problems, students might use pie charts or part-to-whole relationships to visualize and understand the operations involved. Students use logical reasoning to critically evaluate these concepts and representations, assessing their limitations and relevance to the problem at hand.

- **Procedural fluency:** While implementing a solution strategy often requires the fluent use of mathematical procedures, such as calculation or algorithmic steps, logical reasoning is critical in determining these procedures' suitability for the specific problem. This decision-making process might involve choosing between numerical calculation and geometric visualization, depending on which approach offers clearer insights or a more straightforward solution.

- **Monitoring and strategy adjustment:** Throughout the problem-solving process, learners must continually monitor their progress and adjust their approaches as necessary. Logical reasoning plays a key role here, enabling students to pivot their strategies based on the effectiveness of their initial plans. For example, a student solving a multistep geometry problem may need to reconsider their approach if an initial assumption proves incorrect.

Educators can foster the development of these interconnected competencies through thoughtfully designed activities that challenge students to use multiple aspects of their mathematical understanding. An example might involve an elementary classroom activity centered on planning a class fundraising event. Students would need to do the following.

- Calculate potential profits based on different price points for items (using multiplication and estimation).
- Determine optimal quantities to order based on projected sales (applying proportional reasoning).

- Create a budget that accounts for upfront costs and expected revenue (using addition, subtraction, and decimal operations).

Logical reasoning would guide students through critical decision points, such as the following.

- If initial calculations show a loss at certain price points, students would need to reason through why and adjust prices or quantities.
- When comparing different fundraising options, students would evaluate trade-offs between higher-priced items with potentially fewer sales and lower-priced items with potentially greater sales.
- If projected attendance changes, students would need to logically think through how this affects all other variables in their plan.

This example demonstrates how logical reasoning enables students to not just perform calculations but evaluate the reasonableness of their results and make systematic adjustments to their approach based on mathematical evidence.

By engaging students in such comprehensive activities, teachers enhance their ability to apply logical reasoning across different mathematical scenarios, thus strengthening their overall proficiency. This aids students in solving classroom problems and also equips them with the skills to approach future challenges in academic and real-world contexts.

Strategies to Enhance Logical Reasoning and Proof

The following strategies are designed to systematically develop students' capacity for logical reasoning and mathematical proof across grade levels. Each approach supports students in constructing valid arguments, evaluating mathematical claims, and developing precise mathematical communication. While these strategies can be implemented individually, they share common benefits: increasing students' confidence in mathematical reasoning, cultivating their ability to justify solutions, and fostering a deeper understanding of mathematical relationships. At the same time, each strategy offers unique advantages that address specific aspects of logical reasoning and proof, as detailed in the sections that follow.

Socratic Dialogue

The Socratic dialogue method is an effective teaching strategy that employs a question-and-answer format to stimulate critical thinking and illuminate ideas. This pedagogical approach guides students through an in-depth exploration of mathematical concepts by encouraging them to answer probing questions, reflect on their responses, and consider different viewpoints. This process helps students develop a solid understanding of the why behind mathematical facts, rather than simply memorizing formulas or procedures. The following example shares what this method might look like in the context of a high school geometry classroom.

Suppose a high school geometry teacher is introducing the concept of triangle congruence. Instead of directly stating the conditions for triangles to be congruent, the teacher might begin the class with a series of guided questions.

1. **What does it mean for two shapes to be congruent?** This question sets the stage for defining congruence. Students discuss and come to understand that *congruence* implies being identical in shape and size but not necessarily in position.

2. **Can you think of ways to determine whether two triangles are congruent by moving them around? What about if you cannot move them?** Here, students might initially think about physically moving triangles to see whether they match. The teacher can then guide them to consider how they could prove congruence without moving the triangles, leading into a discussion about measurable properties such as side lengths and angles.

3. **If I tell you that two triangles have two sides and the angle between them of equal length and measure, do you think they will be congruent? Why or why not?**
This question introduces the concept of the side-angle-side (SAS) postulate in an engaging way. Students are encouraged to visualize or draw examples and counterexamples, promoting a deeper understanding of the postulate's validity.

4. **Can you think of a situation where two triangles have two angles and a side in common but are not congruent?**
This question challenges students to think critically about the angle-side-angle (ASA) condition and its necessity. The teacher can guide them to consider the importance of the side's position relative to the angles, which solidifies their understanding of congruence conditions.

5. **How can we apply our knowledge of triangle congruence to solve real-world problems? Can you give an example?**
Finally, the teacher prompts students to apply their theoretical knowledge to practical situations, such as engineering problems involving bridges or the design of certain tools. This integrates real-life relevance into the mathematical discussion.

Through this sequence of questions, the teacher leads students through a thoughtful exploration of geometric principles, fostering a classroom environment that values reasoning and understanding over rote memorization. Students learn to articulate their thoughts, justify their reasoning, and engage with mathematical concepts at a profound level.

Indeed, facilitating Socratic dialogue in mathematics has many research-supported benefits. Research by Anita Heijltjes, Tamara van Gog, and Fred Paas (2014) demonstrates that explicit instruction combined with guided dialogue significantly improves students' critical thinking abilities in mathematics. This finding is reinforced by Charles A. Hughes, Jared R. Morris, William J. Therrien, and Sarah K. Benson (2017), whose research shows several key advantages to the Socratic dialogue method.

- **It encourages active participation:** Students show higher engagement levels when they are active participants in the discovery process rather than passive recipients of information.
- **It develops critical thinking:** The method challenges students to think deeply, question continuously, and understand the logic behind mathematical principles, leading to improved problem-solving capabilities.
- **It enhances communication skills:** Regular discussion and explanation improve students' ability to clearly and effectively communicate complex ideas, a key indicator of mathematical proficiency.
- **It fosters deeper understanding:** By focusing on the why and not just the how, students develop a robust understanding of mathematics that goes beyond the classroom, leading to better retention and transfer of mathematical concepts.

These benefits are further supported by Evelyn H. Kroesbergen, Johannes E. H. Van Luit, and Cora J. M. Maas (2004), whose research demonstrates that structured mathematical dialogue leads to improved mathematical achievement compared to traditional instruction methods. Implementing Socratic dialogue requires careful planning and a willingness to adapt to the flow of discussion. However, the benefits of cultivating an environment where students learn to think mathematically and reason logically are immense, making it a powerful tool in the mathematics educator's tool kit.

Error Analysis

Error analysis is a critical teaching strategy that includes engaging students in the examination and discussion of mistakes within mathematical proofs or problem solutions. This method is particularly valuable because it encourages students to think critically about mathematical arguments and understand where reasoning can go awry.

By identifying errors and considering how to correct them, students not only enhance their problem-solving skills but also deepen their understanding of the mathematical concepts involved. The following is a relevant example from a middle school classroom.

Imagine a middle school teacher working with students on solving equations. The teacher presents the class with a solved example that intentionally includes an error.

Given problem: $2x + 5 = 15$

Student's solution: $2x + 5 - 5 = 15 - 5$

$2x = 10$

$x = 10 \div 2$

$x = 6$ (An error is intentionally included here.)

Instead of simply correcting the mistake, the teacher uses it for an error analysis session by asking the class to review the solution and identify any errors. Students discuss in pairs or small groups to pinpoint where the error occurred and why it is an error, focusing on each step of the solution process.

1. **Identify the error:** Students might notice that the final division was done incorrectly; $10 \div 2$ should obviously result in 5, not 6. Discussing this helps students understand the importance of doing careful calculations and checking their work.

2. **Discuss the impact:** The teacher guides students to explore how this error affects the solution of the equation, emphasizing accuracy in every step. This way, students understand that even a single small error can lead to incorrect conclusions.

3. **Correct and justify:** The teacher then asks students to correct the error and justify the correct steps. This involves performing the arithmetic correctly as well as explaining why each step is necessary and how it contributes to solving the equation.

4. **Generalize the learning:** The teacher encourages students to think about general strategies for avoiding similar errors, such as double-checking each arithmetic operation and verifying the solution by substituting it back into the original equation.

Benefits of error analysis are well documented in research. A study by Rittle-Johnson (2017) demonstrates that structured error analysis significantly contributes to mathematics learning outcomes. Its benefits include the following.

- **It promotes a growth mindset:** Research by Li and Bates (2020) shows that when students learn to view errors as learning opportunities rather than failures, they develop more adaptive responses to mathematical challenges. In this way, students learn that errors are a natural part of the learning process and that valuable insights can be gained by understanding and correcting them.

- **It enhances critical thinking:** Powell and colleagues' (2020) synthesis of mathematics interventions shows that systematic error analysis leads to improved mathematical reasoning. Analyzing errors requires students to think deeply about the logic of their mathematical processes, which sharpens their analytical skills.

- **It improves problem-solving strategies:** A study by Schneider and Stern (2010) demonstrates that by regularly identifying and correcting errors, students develop more reliable problem-solving techniques and learn to approach problems more strategically. This research shows that a systematic approach to error analysis contributes to more flexible mathematical thinking.

- **It builds confidence:** As documented by Maria Chiara Passolunghi, Elisa Cargnelutti, and Sandra Pellizzoni (2019), when students become more adept at spotting and correcting their mistakes, they gain confidence in their ability to tackle complex mathematical challenges. This research links improved error detection abilities with reduced mathematics anxiety and increased self-efficacy.

Incorporating error analysis into the curriculum is a practical way to enhance students' engagement with mathematics. It transforms errors from mere setbacks to powerful learning opportunities, which encourages students to approach mathematics with curiosity and resilience. By making error analysis a regular part of the classroom routine, teachers help students become more proficient and confident mathematicians.

Analytical Discussion

Encouraging analytical discussion in the classroom is a vital teaching strategy, particularly in mathematics, where understanding the reasoning behind solutions is as important as the solutions themselves. In an environment that promotes open discussion and critique of logical processes, students can deepen their comprehension of mathematical concepts and enhance their problem-solving skills. The following related example is from an elementary classroom.

Consider a fourth-grade class learning about fractions. Instead of simply teaching the procedures for adding fractions, the teacher can engage students in a more interactive and analytical exploration of the topic.

- **Activity:** Comparing fractions
- **Objective:** Students will learn to add fractions and understand the reasons behind the addition process, focusing on how to find common denominators.
- **Task:** The teacher presents a problem where students need to find the sum of $\frac{1}{3}$ and $\frac{1}{4}$. Instead of leading directly to the solution, the teacher encourages a discussion about different ways to approach the problem.

Steps for Encouraging Analytical Discussion

1. **Initial thoughts:** Students first share their initial thoughts on how to solve the problem. Some might suggest converting fractions to decimals, while others might prefer finding a common denominator.
2. **Group exploration:** Students work in small groups to explore their chosen methods. One group might use visual aids like fraction bars or pie charts to find a common denominator, while another might attempt to apply a rule they remember about equivalent fractions.

3. **Presentation of methods:** Each group presents their method and findings to the class. They explain why they chose their approach and how they believe it worked for adding the fractions.

4. **Class discussion:** After each presentation, the teacher facilitates a class discussion where students can ask questions, point out potential flaws, or suggest improvements. The teacher encourages students to think about why certain methods are effective and how different approaches might be used in different situations.

5. **Consolidation:** The teacher summarizes the discussion, highlights the importance of finding a common denominator for adding fractions, and emphasizes the value of using visual aids to understand how different fractions relate to each other.

6. **Reflection:** Finally, students reflect on what they learned from the discussion. They might journal about how their understanding of fraction addition has changed or discuss how they could apply these strategies to future problems.

Benefits of analytical discussion in mathematics are well documented through research. Studies synthesized by Powell and colleagues (2020) demonstrate the following advantages.

- **Enhanced understanding:** Rittle-Johnson and Schneider (2015) show that discussing different methods and critiquing solutions help students grasp the why and how of mathematical processes, not just the what. Their research indicates that verbal explanation and discussion lead to deeper conceptual understanding.

- **Critical thinking development:** Research by Heijltjes and colleagues (2014) demonstrates that regularly engaging in analytical discussions encourages students to think critically about mathematics, questioning assumptions and exploring alternatives. These findings show significant improvements in critical thinking when students participate in structured mathematical discourse.

- **Improved communication skills:** A literature review by Jiwon Hwang and Paul J. Riccomini (2016) indicates that articulating their reasoning and listening to others strengthen students' mathematical communication skills, which are essential for clearly expressing complex ideas. This research also links mathematical discourse to improved problem-solving abilities.

- **Increased engagement:** Morgan and colleagues (2015) find that when students actively discuss and solve problems, their engagement with the subject matter increases, making learning more dynamic and enjoyable. This research shows higher achievement levels in classrooms that prioritize mathematical discussion.

- **Collaborative skills:** According to Marjorie Montague (2007), working together to analyze problems and discuss solutions teaches students valuable collaboration skills that prepare them for group work in later educational settings and in life. Montague's findings demonstrate that collaborative mathematical discourse supports both individual and group learning outcomes.

By integrating activities that require analytical discussion, you can foster a classroom environment that values deep understanding and critical examination of mathematical concepts. This approach not only aids students in mastering the subject matter but also equips them with the intellectual tools necessary for thoughtful analysis and problem solving in all areas of their education.

Diverse Proof Techniques

Integrating diverse proof techniques into the mathematics curriculum is a critical strategy for developing students' adaptability in handling complex mathematical concepts. When you teach various types of proof techniques, such as direct proof, indirect proof, and proof by contradiction, students gain a richer understanding of how mathematical arguments can be structured and validated. This exposure helps them solve problems as well as think critically about the nature of proof itself. The following example of this method is in the context of a middle school classroom.

Consider a middle school classroom where the teacher introduces students to different proof techniques through a series of targeted lessons and activities.

- **Activity:** Understanding different proof techniques
- **Objective:** Students will learn to apply different proof techniques to validate mathematical statements, enhancing their ability to think logically and abstractly.

Examples of Proof Techniques

1. **Direct proof**
    - *Concept introduction*—Explain that direct proof involves proving a statement by direct application of axioms, definitions, and previously established theorems.
    - *Example task*—Prove that the sum of two even numbers is always even. Students can start by letting the two even numbers be represented as $2a$ and $2b$ (where a and b are integers) and show that their sum, $2a + 2b$, can be factored to $2(a + b)$, which is clearly an even number.

2. **Indirect proof (proof by contrapositive)**
    - *Concept introduction*—Teach that in indirect proof, especially proof by contrapositive, the strategy is to prove that if the conclusion is false, then the premise must be false as well.
    - *Example task*—Prove that if the product of two numbers is odd, then both numbers must be odd. Students assume the contrapositive: If at least one number is even, then the product is even. And they thus indirectly verify the original statement.

3. **Proof by contradiction**
    - *Concept introduction*—Explain that proof by contradiction involves assuming the opposite of the statement to be proven and showing that this assumption leads to a contradiction.

> • *Example task*—Prove that there is no greatest even number. Students assume there is a greatest even number, say $2n$. They can then show that $2n + 2$ is also an even number and greater than $2n$, leading to a contradiction.

Review the following five steps for teaching proof techniques.

1. **Introduce concepts:** Begin with clear definitions and discuss the logical underpinnings of each proof technique. Use visual aids and simple examples to illustrate how each method works.

2. **Offer guided practice:** Provide students with structured exercises to apply each proof technique. Start with simple problems and gradually introduce more complex scenarios to deepen their understanding.

3. **Facilitate group discussions:** Encourage students to work in groups to tackle proof problems. This fosters collaborative learning and allows students to debate and reason through the proofs together, which enhances comprehension.

4. **Apply the techniques to new situations:** Challenge students to use these proof techniques in new or unfamiliar mathematical contexts. This could involve proving statements about geometric shapes, algebraic expressions, or number theory.

5. **Prioritize reflection and feedback:** Have students reflect on their learning process and the challenges they faced. Provide feedback on their proofs, highlighting logical rigor and creativity in their approaches.

The benefits of teaching diverse proof techniques are well documented in research. Research by Schneider and Stern (2010) demonstrates the following advantages.

- **Enhanced logical thinking:** Heijltjes and colleagues' (2014) research shows that learning different ways to approach proofs strengthens students' logical reasoning abilities, crucial for academic success in mathematics and other disciplines. Their study demonstrates that significant improvements in analytical thinking occur when students are exposed to multiple proof methods.

- **Greater flexibility:** Studies by Schneider and colleagues (2011) indicate that exposure to multiple proof techniques makes students more adaptable in solving problems, as they can choose the most appropriate method for each situation. This research links procedural flexibility with improved mathematical outcomes.

- **Deeper understanding of mathematics:** According to Rittle-Johnson (2017), understanding why a mathematical statement is true, rather than just knowing it is true, deepens students' overall understanding of mathematics. This finding is supported by evidence showing that students who understand proofs demonstrate better conceptual knowledge.

- **Improved problem-solving skills:** Powell and colleagues (2020) document how the skills developed through learning various proof techniques are transferable to many areas of study and problem-solving scenarios outside of mathematics. Their synthesis shows that systematic instruction in mathematical reasoning leads to improved problem-solving capabilities across domains.

By incorporating diverse proof techniques into the mathematics curriculum, educators equip students with a comprehensive tool kit for understanding and demonstrating mathematical truths, preparing them for more advanced studies and diverse intellectual challenges.

Construction of Logical Arguments

The construction of logical arguments can be effectively implemented in an elementary classroom through activities that blend mathematical reasoning with real-world applications. This method encourages students to think critically about everyday situations, which enhances their ability to articulate and defend their mathematical decisions. The following example is from an elementary classroom.

- **Activity:** Allocating playtime in different activity stations
- **Objective:** Students will apply division and fairness concepts to equally distribute playtime among activity stations, fostering their ability to construct and justify logical arguments.
- **Example task:** The teacher sets up three activity stations in the classroom—(1) a drawing station, (2) a reading corner, and (3) a puzzle table. With 45 minutes available, the class must decide how to allocate the time among the stations so that all students can engage in each activity.

Steps for Teaching Logical Argument Construction

1. **Problem introduction:** Clearly present the scenario—"There are three stations and 45 minutes of playtime. How can we divide the time so that students can enjoy all the activities equally?" Prompt students to consider what factors might influence their decision, such as the number of students interested in each activity and the engagement time typically needed at each station.

2. **Student proposals:** Invite groups of students to suggest different methods of time allocation. One group might propose equally dividing the time among the stations, giving 15 minutes to each. Another group might suggest varying the time based on perceived interest or activity complexity, such as 20 minutes for puzzles, 15 minutes for drawing, and 10 minutes for reading.

3. **Argument construction:** Have each student or group explain why their method is fair and beneficial. They must use logical reasoning to support their proposal, considering aspects like equal opportunity, interest levels, and practicality of switching stations. Encourage students to use expressions like "equally divided," "more time because . . .," and "less time since . . ." to clearly articulate their reasoning.

4. **Class debate:** Organize a structured debate where each group presents their argument and responds to questions or critiques from their peers. This interactive discussion allows students to challenge and refine their thinking. Emphasize respectful listening and questioning as they evaluate different viewpoints and the logic behind them.

5. **Reflection on reasoning:** Conclude with a reflection session where students discuss what they learned from hearing different arguments. Highlight the importance of backing up decisions with sound reasoning and the impact of well-thought-out arguments.

6. **Reinforcement through practice:** Extend this exercise by introducing more complex scenarios or incorporating variables, like unexpected interruptions or the introduction of a new station, which will prompt students to rethink and adjust their original allocations.

The benefits of promoting logical argument construction are well established through research. Studies synthesized by Powell and colleagues (2020) demonstrate the following advantages.

- **Enhanced analytical skills:** Heijltjes and colleagues' (2014) research shows that students develop stronger analytical abilities as they assess various factors influencing their decisions and they learn to weigh different elements and foresee potential outcomes. Their findings indicate that structured practice in logical argumentation leads to improved analytical thinking.

- **Deepened understanding of fairness:** Studies by Morgan and colleagues (2015) demonstrate that through these discussions, students explore the concept of fairness as not just equal but adjusted sharing based on reasoned criteria, which enriches their moral and ethical development. This research links mathematical discourse to improved conceptual understanding of proportional reasoning.

- **Boosted engagement:** According to Montague (2007), engaging in debates about familiar, enjoyable activities ensures high student interest and investment in the learning process. Montague's (2007) research shows that contextualized mathematical arguments lead to increased student participation and motivation.

- **Skill development in adaptability:** Schneider and colleagues (2011) document how experience with mathematical argumentation enhances students' ability to flexibly adjust their thinking. Their findings demonstrate that students learn to adapt their arguments and strategies in response to new information or changing conditions, a crucial skill for academic and life success.

By integrating these strategies into classrooms, teachers can significantly boost students' ability to use logical reasoning and proof. These skills are essential for students' academic success in mathematics as well as for their empowerment as logical thinkers who can apply their knowledge to solve real-world problems.

Conclusion

As we conclude our exploration of logical reasoning and proof within the CMC framework, it's clear that this competency is not merely a series of activities or one-off strategies but an essential tool for nurturing deep mathematical understanding and cognitive agility. Logical reasoning and the construction of proofs embody the essence of mathematical thinking—transforming abstract concepts into tangible and verifiable truths.

Our role as teachers transcends teaching students to solve equations or memorize theorems; it involves cultivating a mindset that appreciates the rigor and beauty of logical consistency and the power of well-founded argumentation. This competency equips students for mathematical pursuits in school and also prepares them to face real-world problems with a structured and analytical approach.

Moreover, integrating logical reasoning and proof throughout the curriculum ensures that students develop a balanced set of skills. They learn to perform mathematical operations and to understand and articulate the reasons behind their choices and solutions. In this chapter, we've seen how adaptive reasoning seamlessly interacts with problem solving and conceptual understanding, forming a robust framework that supports and enhances students' mathematical capabilities. Through carefully designed classroom activities and thoughtful pedagogical strategies, we can help students build strong logical foundations and reasoning skills. These skills are crucial for succeeding academically and for navigating the complexities of an increasingly data-driven world.

CHAPTER 5

Communication and Representation

In our exploration of the CMC framework, consider the pivotal roles of communication and representation. This chapter considers how effective communication and diverse mathematical representations are essential for enhancing understanding as well as for expressing complex mathematical ideas with clarity and precision. These elements are vital for transforming abstract mathematical thoughts into understandable concepts that students can share and discuss.

Communication in mathematics involves more than just the ability to express numbers or formulas; it encompasses the articulation of reasoning, the explanation of problem-solving methods, and the justification of conclusions. Effective mathematical communication ensures that students can clearly convey their own ideas and fully grasp the ideas of others, facilitating deeper communal engagement with mathematical concepts. Similarly, the use of varied mathematical representations—such as symbols, diagrams, graphs, and physical models—plays a crucial role in how students understand and interact with mathematical concepts. These representations provide different lenses through which students can view mathematical ideas, making them accessible to students with diverse learning styles and strengths.

While Anna Sfard's (2001) foundational work first established the importance of peer explanation in mathematics learning, further research has since substantially reinforced these findings. A synthesis of mathematics interventions by Powell and colleagues (2020) demonstrates that students who regularly explain their mathematical thinking to peers show significant improvements in both understanding and retention. This finding is further supported by Hwang and Riccomini (2016), whose research reveals that peer-to-peer mathematical communication enhances both conceptual understanding and procedural fluency. Additionally, Morgan and colleagues (2015) find that classrooms emphasizing mathematical discourse and peer explanation show higher levels of student achievement and concept retention.

By emphasizing these elements within the CMC framework, we aim to enable students to clearly articulate their mathematical thinking and also to develop a robust ability to interpret and engage with others' mathematical expressions. This dual focus on communication and representation equips students with the tools necessary for academic success and lays the groundwork for their future endeavors in any mathematics-related field. The following sections explore the essence of communication and representation before reviewing strategies to cultivate these skills and thereby ensure that students can navigate the complexities of mathematical dialogue and representation with confidence.

The Essence of Communication and Representation

In mathematics, communication and representation are deeply intertwined and support students' development. While communication involves the clear expression and interpretation of mathematical ideas through verbal, written, symbolic, and visual forms, representation provides the tools through which we make abstract mathematical concepts tangible and understandable. Together, these elements ensure that students grasp mathematical concepts and can effectively share and discuss them with others.

Representations are fundamental to understanding mathematics due to mathematics' inherently abstract nature. Indeed, our engagement with mathematical concepts is mediated entirely through various forms of representations. These representations allow us to visualize and manipulate mathematical ideas that would otherwise be intangible. Research by Powell and colleagues (2020) demonstrates that successful mathematics instruction consistently incorporates multiple representations to support student understanding and communication of mathematical ideas.

The essence of learning and doing mathematics transcends the mere acquisition of facts and procedural knowledge; it fundamentally involves learning how to interpret and utilize representations to comprehend and communicate mathematical ideas. For instance, the concept of number systems, foundational to all mathematics, heavily relies on our ability to represent numbers and operations in multiple ways—from number lines and dot arrays to symbolic equations and graphical displays. Studies by Morgan and colleagues (2015) show that students who regularly engage with various representations and communicate their mathematical thinking demonstrate stronger conceptual understanding and problem-solving abilities.

Development of Communication and Representation Skills

The development of strong communication and representation skills requires systematic attention to how students learn to express mathematical ideas and use various representations effectively. Research by Powell and colleagues (2020) demonstrates that this development typically follows a progression from concrete to abstract representations while building students' capacity to clearly and precisely communicate mathematical thinking.

Progressive Development of Representations

Physical representations play a pivotal role in early mathematics education, serving as vital tools for communication, conceptual thinking, and computation. For elementary students (grades K–3), manipulatives like base-ten blocks and number lines provide concrete ways to explore mathematical relationships. As students progress to upper elementary and middle school grades (4–8), they begin transitioning to more abstract representations while maintaining connections to concrete models. By high school, students should be able to move flexibly between concrete and abstract representations, choosing the most appropriate form for each mathematical situation.

This reliance on representations is not just a pedagogical tool but a necessity for the development of mathematical thinking. By providing students with diverse representations, we enable them to see mathematical concepts from different perspectives, thereby enhancing their ability to apply these concepts in various contexts.

Physical representations facilitate shared understanding and preservation of concepts by externalizing personal mathematical ideas, making them accessible and tangible for learners. These representations clarify complex ideas, enhance reasoning, and deepen comprehension across a wide array of mathematical topics.

The use of physical models, such as manipulatives, diagrams, or interactive simulations, allows students to visualize and manipulate mathematical concepts physically. This hands-on approach is particularly beneficial in making abstract ideas more concrete. For instance, students can grasp place value and arithmetic operations by physically grouping, rearranging, and regrouping base-ten blocks to represent sums and differences. This method can transform a student's abstract understanding of numbers into a more concrete and relatable concept.

Furthermore, physical representations are instrumental in developing and refining efficient algorithms for basic operations. They provide a tactile method for understanding the steps involved in calculation processes. For example, an abacus can be used to teach students addition and subtraction through a process of sliding beads. This helps them both understand the operation itself and develop a mental map of the algorithm that underpins it. Similarly, fraction strips can be used to demonstrate how different fractions relate to each other, supporting the algorithms for fraction addition and subtraction.

These representations are not just tools for learning existing concepts; they also spur the creation of new mathematical ideas and methods. By engaging with physical models, students can experiment with patterns, test hypotheses, and develop new strategies for problem solving. This exploratory approach encourages deeper engagement with mathematics, prompting students to ask questions, seek out patterns, and connect concepts in novel ways.

By integrating physical representations into mathematics teaching and learning, educators can provide students with a powerful arsenal of tools that facilitate understanding of complex concepts as well as cultivate an environment where mathematical ideas can flourish. These tools empower students to communicate and reason mathematically, laying a strong foundation for deeper academic exploration and practical application in their future educational and professional endeavors.

For example, in kindergarten and first grade (ages five to seven), students begin working with physical objects like counters or blocks to understand addition and subtraction concretely. Second-grade students (ages seven to eight) continue using these manipulatives while transitioning to more abstract representations, beginning to connect the physical models to written numerical expressions. By third grade (ages eight to nine), students should be comfortable moving between concrete manipulatives and symbolic notation, primarily using physical models to explore new concepts or verify their thinking. As students mature, these physical models can be transitioned into more abstract representations such as number lines or algebraic symbols, which offer more flexibility in handling complex mathematical problems. Similarly, visual models like graphs or diagrams can help bridge the gap between concrete operations and abstract algebraic expressions, showing students how mathematical concepts evolve and connect across different areas of study.

Moreover, effective use of representations aids in critical thinking and problem solving. It encourages students to question how different representations relate to each other and how each can be used to solve problems. For instance, in exploring number systems, students might use base-ten blocks to physically manipulate and understand place value, which is a cornerstone of our numeral system. They could then relate these physical manipulations to more abstract decimal and fractional representations, deepening their conceptual understanding.

Thus, by integrating a rich array of mathematical representations into teaching practices, educators make abstract concepts accessible and equip students with the skills to think mathematically and solve problems creatively. This approach not only clarifies complex ideas but also enriches students' mathematical experiences, preparing them for further education and everyday life, where mathematics plays a crucial role.

Mathematical concepts are significantly enriched by using multiple representations, which are much more than just visual aids or teaching strategies; they are integral to the fabric of mathematical content itself and play a crucial role in fostering mathematical reasoning. For example, the numeral 847 is not merely a sequence of digits but a representation that encapsulates substantial mathematical thought and interpretation.

Multiple representations, including visual models, symbols, diagrams, and verbal descriptions, enable learners to grasp complex mathematical ideas by providing different perspectives on the same concept. This variety doesn't just accommodate diverse learning styles; it deepens understanding by highlighting different aspects of a concept. For instance, a quadratic equation can be represented algebraically, graphed as a parabola in a coordinate plane, or discussed in the context of real-world applications such as projectile motion. Each representation gives unique insights and aids in understanding the underlying mathematical relationships.

Research underscores the importance of these representations in learning. While Shaaron Ainsworth's (2006) work establishes foundational principles about multiple representations, other studies have substantially expanded our understanding of their impact. Powell and colleagues (2020) demonstrate through their synthesis of mathematics interventions that multiple representations are crucial for developing robust mathematical understanding, particularly when they provide complementary information and help prevent misconceptions. This finding is reinforced by Morgan and colleagues (2015), whose research shows that students achieve better outcomes when instruction incorporates various representational forms. Additionally, Hwang and Riccomini (2016) find that combining visual, symbolic, and verbal representations significantly enhances students' mathematical comprehension and retention. Their research particularly emphasizes how integrating different representational forms helps students develop deeper conceptual understanding and transfer knowledge more effectively across mathematical contexts.

Moreover, multiple representations are not just static images or fixed symbols; they are dynamic tools for exploration and discovery in mathematics. For example, dynamic geometry software allows students to manipulate geometric figures to actively explore properties and theorems. This interaction can lead to a deeper understanding and appreciation of geometry as students see the immediate effects of transformations or adjustments to figures.

In the classroom, educators can harness the power of multiple representations by encouraging students to translate mathematical problems into different forms. For instance, converting a complex word problem into an algebraic equation, a table of values, and a graph can help students see the relationships between the variables and better understand the problem's structure. This practice not only enhances problem-solving skills but also encourages critical thinking about which representations are most effective for different types of problems and why.

Thus, multiple representations are essential for understanding mathematical concepts and for applying these concepts. They bridge the gap between abstract mathematical theories and practical applications, making mathematics more accessible and meaningful to students. By integrating these diverse forms into teaching, educators can cultivate a richer, more connected understanding of mathematics, preparing students to use these skills in their academic pursuits and everyday problem solving.

For us to use numbers effectively, communicate about them, or manipulate them, they must be named and structured in a way that we can universally understand and apply them. We use decimal place-value notation in daily life and commerce; this system facilitates basic transactions and underpins complex mathematical and scientific computations.

In the decimal system, each digit in a number has a place value depending on its position, and these positions are based on powers of ten. This structure allows for clear representation and manipulation of numbers, regardless of their size. For example, the number 423 is understood through this system by recognizing that the 4 represents four hundreds, the 2 stands for two tens, and the 3 signifies three ones.

Using base-ten blocks can be highly effective in teaching this concept, especially for visual and tactile learners. These blocks, which represent units, tens, hundreds, and thousands, provide a physical and visual way of understanding the decomposition of numbers into their constituent parts.

The number 423 can be detailed as:

$$423 = 400 + 20 + 3$$
$$423 = (4 \times 100) + (2 \times 10) + (3 \times 1)$$
$$423 = (4 \times 10^2) + (2 \times 10^1) + (3 \times 10^0)$$

This representation emphasizes the role of each digit in the number according to its position, where 10^2 represents hundreds, 10^1 represents tens, and 10^0 represents units.

Exploring a larger number, such as 75,862, helps illustrate how this system works seamlessly for larger scales.

The number 75,862 can be expressed in its expanded form as:

$$75{,}862 = (7 \times 10{,}000) + (5 \times 1{,}000) + (8 \times 100) + (6 \times 10) + (2 \times 1)$$
$$75{,}862 = (7 \times 10^4) + (5 \times 10^3) + (8 \times 10^2) + (6 \times 10^1) + (2 \times 10^0)$$

Each component of this breakdown corresponds to a power of ten determined by the position of the digit, demonstrating how every number within the decimal system is an accumulation of powers of ten, each multiplied by a digit from 0 to 9. This system simplifies the teaching and learning of arithmetic, as well as ensures a common understanding that supports basic education and the intricate requirements of commerce, technology, and science.

By utilizing both symbolic notation and concrete tools like base-ten blocks in education, teachers can greatly enhance students' numerical literacy. These methods fortify understanding of the decimal system's logic and utility, empowering students to confidently handle numbers across various applications, from everyday counting to advanced mathematical problem solving.

Criteria for Effective Representations

When selecting and implementing mathematical representations, educators must consider several key characteristics that influence their effectiveness. Research by Powell and colleagues (2020) demonstrates that carefully chosen representations based on specific criteria, including visibility, streamlining, adaptability, and precision, lead to better mathematical understanding and communication.

Visibility

How clearly does the representation disclose the core concept? This criterion evaluates whether the representation enables students to intuitively grasp the underlying mathematical ideas. For elementary students in grades 1–3, fraction circles dramatically enhance the visibility of fraction concepts, making it easier to understand parts of a whole compared to simply presenting fractions as numerical values or on a number line. This tangible format can significantly clarify the concept of fractions for young learners. By fourth and fifth grade, students can transition to more abstract representations while maintaining connections to these visual models. On the other hand, abstract symbols like fraction notations ($\frac{1}{2}$, $\frac{3}{4}$, and so on) require careful scaffolding and explicit connections to visual models, as they don't inherently show how fractions relate to one another in size or scale.

Streamlining

How effectively does the representation facilitate straightforward and concise communication of ideas? Streamlining evaluates whether a representation simplifies the communication process, making it more direct and less cumbersome. Symbolic representations, such as algebraic expressions, are highly streamlined, enabling efficient communication of complex mathematical ideas, particularly in higher levels of mathematics and formal written contexts. For example, secondary students can use mathematical symbols to express patterns and relationships that would be cumbersome to describe in words alone.

Adaptability

How flexibly does the representation apply to a variety of mathematical concepts? This criterion considers the versatility of the representation across different areas of mathematics. While methods like using fingers for counting provide initial accessibility for primary-grade students, they lack broad adaptability. In contrast, the number line and the decimal system exhibit high adaptability, capable of representing a wide spectrum of mathematical concepts, from whole numbers to real numbers. Students in middle and high school particularly benefit from representations that can be applied across different mathematical domains.

Precision

How accurately does the representation convey the intended mathematical concept? Precision involves the clarity and exactness with which a representation communicates ideas. Effective representations are precise and unambiguous, often established by common usage within education and mathematical communities. This ensures that learners can apply the concepts correctly without misinterpretation. As students progress through grade levels, the precision of their mathematical representations should increase, moving from informal to more formal mathematical notation.

How to Implement These Criteria in Instructional Practices

Research by Morgan and colleagues (2015) demonstrates that effective implementation of these criteria requires thoughtful attention to developmental progression and active engagement strategies. The following grade-level considerations help teachers apply these criteria systematically.

- **In early grades:** Using counters or blocks can enhance the visibility of basic arithmetic operations, making abstract concepts tangible.

- **In middle grades:** Diagrams or graphs can streamline understanding of functions and relationships, making them less abstract and more accessible.

- **In high school and advanced mathematics:** Algebraic and calculus concepts benefit from the adaptability of symbolic notation, allowing for precise and efficient manipulation of complex expressions.

By focusing on visibility, streamlining, adaptability, and precision, educators can select and utilize mathematical representations that not only make abstract concepts accessible but also foster deeper understanding and more effective communication of mathematics. This approach ensures that students are equipped with the tools necessary for both academic success and practical application, enhancing their overall mathematical literacy and problem-solving skills.

Before we delve into specific strategies to enhance communication and representation in mathematics education, it is crucial to understand how these foundational concepts translate into effective teaching practices. The essence of communication and representation within the CMC framework involves transforming how students interact with mathematical ideas to make these concepts more accessible and engaging. Students need to engage with physical and visual representations to grasp abstract mathematical concepts; in practice, teachers facilitate this understanding by incorporating manipulatives, digital tools, and real-world contexts into lessons. This allows students to explore and manipulate concepts physically and visually, such as using geometric construction sets to build shapes and explore their properties, which helps elementary students understand geometry in a hands-on manner.

Additionally, effective communication in mathematics means moving from passive learning to active engagement. Rather than just listening or watching, it requires active participation. Teachers implement activities that require students to explain their reasoning, debate mathematical ideas, and present their solutions to the class. This approach reinforces their learning as well as enhances their ability to communicate mathematical ideas clearly and confidently.

Moreover, while mathematics is often perceived as a solitary activity, communication and representation thrive in collaborative environments, marking a transition from individual understanding to collaborative insight. Teachers create opportunities for group work where students can discuss problems, share different methods of solving them, and collectively develop representations. These opportunities could include collaborative projects where students use statistical methods to analyze class data, interpret results, and present findings using various representations, such as graphs, charts, and reports. In transitioning to discussing specific strategies, keep in mind that these approaches are designed to build on the foundational knowledge discussed and to further bridge the gap between understanding concepts and effectively applying them in diverse contexts.

This implementation approach ensures that students develop individual proficiency and collaborative mathematical discourse skills while working with increasingly sophisticated representations.

How to Build Mathematical Communication

The ability to effectively communicate mathematical ideas develops alongside students' understanding of various representations. Morgan and colleagues (2015) demonstrate that when students regularly engage in mathematical discourse about different representations, they develop stronger mathematical reasoning and communication skills. This development involves the following.

- **Progressive vocabulary development:** Build from informal mathematical language to precise mathematical terminology.
- **Multiple modes of expression:** Practice communicating mathematical ideas verbally, in writing, and through various representations.
- **Justification skills:** Learn to explain mathematical thinking and defend mathematical arguments using appropriate representations.
- **Translation abilities:** Develop facility in moving between different representations and explaining their relationships.

This systematic attention to both representation and communication supports students in developing comprehensive mathematical proficiency that extends beyond procedural knowledge to deep conceptual understanding.

The development of mathematical communication skills is a progressive journey that parallels students' growing understanding of mathematical representations. According to Morgan and colleagues (2015), when students regularly engage in mathematical discourse about different representations, they build stronger mathematical reasoning and communication skills. Hwang and Riccomini (2016) further demonstrate that explicit instruction in mathematical communication leads to deeper conceptual understanding and improved problem-solving abilities.

Progressive Vocabulary Development

Students' mathematical vocabulary develops through distinct stages.

- **Informal language (grades K–2):** Students begin by describing mathematical concepts in everyday terms, such as saying *splitting into equal parts* before learning the term *division*.

- **Transitional language (grades 3–5):** Students start incorporating formal mathematical terms while still connecting the terms to familiar language.
- **Precise mathematical terms (grades 6–12):** Students increasingly use standard mathematical vocabulary to communicate ideas accurately and efficiently.

Multiple Modes of Expression

Effective mathematical communication involves various modes.

- **Verbal communication:** Students learn the following skills.
  - Clearly explaining their mathematical thinking
  - Using appropriate mathematical terminology
  - Participating in mathematical discussions
  - Presenting solutions to peers
- **Written communication:** Students develop skills in the following.
  - Recording mathematical procedures
  - Explaining problem-solving strategies
  - Writing mathematical arguments
  - Creating mathematical explanations for others
- **Visual communication:** Students become proficient in the following.
  - Creating diagrams and drawings to represent problems
  - Using mathematical symbols appropriately
  - Developing graphic organizers for mathematical concepts
  - Interpreting visual mathematical representations

Justification Skills

Research by Heijltjes and colleagues (2014) shows that the ability to justify mathematical thinking is crucial for deeper understanding. Students learn to do the following.

Communication and Representation 109

- Support their solutions with logical arguments.
- Explain why their strategies work.
- Identify and correct errors in mathematical reasoning.
- Evaluate the effectiveness of different approaches.

Translation Abilities

Powell and colleagues (2020) emphasize the importance of students' ability to move between different representations. This includes the following.

- Converting between verbal descriptions and mathematical symbols
- Translating between concrete and abstract representations
- Moving between different mathematical representations (graphs, tables, equations, and so on)
- Choosing appropriate representations for specific situations

Classroom Implementation

To support the development of these communication skills, teachers should do the following.

- Model clear mathematical communication.
- Provide regular opportunities for mathematical discussion.
- Require written explanations of mathematical thinking.
- Use structured protocols for mathematical discourse.
- Incorporate both formal and informal opportunities for mathematical communication.

Assessment Considerations

Effective assessment of mathematical communication includes the following.

- Rubrics that evaluate both content and clarity
- Opportunities for both written and verbal communication

- Assessment of students' ability to use multiple representations
- Evaluation of students' justification skills

By systematically developing these communication skills alongside representational abilities, students become more proficient in expressing mathematical ideas and engaging in mathematical discourse. This comprehensive approach supports deeper mathematical understanding and prepares students for increasingly complex mathematical tasks.

Interplay Between Communication and Representation and Other Competencies

The ability to communicate mathematically and use varied representations enhances all other competencies within the CMC framework. Research by Rittle-Johnson (2017) demonstrates that strong communication skills and flexible use of representations are critical factors in developing overall mathematical proficiency.

As discussed in chapter 2 (page 25), multiple representations support both conceptual understanding and procedural fluency. Schneider and colleagues (2011) show that when students can move flexibly between different representations, they develop deeper conceptual understanding while also strengthening their procedural skills. For example, when learning fraction multiplication, students might use area models to understand the concept (supporting conceptual understanding) while also practicing the standard algorithm (developing procedural fluency). This dual approach, supported by research from Powell and colleagues (2020), leads to more robust mathematics learning.

Problem solving and modeling (chapter 3, page 47) rely heavily on students' ability to represent problems in various ways and communicate their solution strategies. Studies by Hwang and Riccomini (2016) demonstrate that students who can effectively translate between verbal descriptions, visual representations, and mathematical symbols show greater success in problem solving. For instance, when approaching word problems, successful students typically do the following.

- Translate verbal descriptions into mathematical representations.
- Select and use appropriate solution methods.
- Clearly communicate their reasoning to justify their solutions.

Logical reasoning and proof (chapter 4, page 71) become more accessible when students can represent their thinking through multiple modes. According to Heijltjes and colleagues (2014), the ability to clearly communicate mathematical arguments and represent them in various ways strengthens students' capacity for logical reasoning. For example, geometric proofs often combine verbal explanations with visual representations to construct valid arguments; this allows students to better demonstrate their reasoning.

The strategic use of tools (chapter 6, page 121) is enhanced when students can communicate about and represent their mathematical thinking using various tools. Morgan and colleagues (2015) find that students who can articulate their choices about different representations and tools demonstrate greater mathematical competence. This relationship highlights how communication and representation skills support students in making strategic decisions about when and how to use different mathematical tools and representations.

Strategies to Enhance Communication and Representation

The competency of communication and representation is pivotal for deepening students' understanding and ability to convey complex mathematical ideas. Effective communication in mathematics goes beyond mere numerical or formulaic expression; it involves explaining concepts clearly, justifying reasoning, and translating mathematical thoughts across various forms and contexts. Similarly, adept representation encompasses the ability to visualize and manipulate mathematical concepts through different media and formats, bridging the gap between abstract ideas and tangible understanding.

To foster this competency, you can implement a range of strategies designed to enhance both how students express mathematical ideas and how they interpret the representations of these ideas. These strategies are instrumental in creating a learning environment where students deeply engage with mathematics and develop the skills necessary to confidently articulate and visualize mathematical concepts. The following sections outline practical approaches and activities that teachers can incorporate across elementary, middle, and high school levels to cultivate these vital skills.

Encourage Varied Forms of Expression

Encouraging varied forms of expression in mathematics education is essential, as it enables students to explore and grasp concepts from multiple perspectives. By allowing students to explain mathematical ideas in their own words, create visual representations, and translate between different forms—such as converting algebraic expressions into graphical depictions—educators can significantly deepen their students' understanding and engagement with mathematical concepts. This multifaceted approach reinforces learning through repetition in various formats, and it makes connections between different mathematical domains more apparent. The following examples describe how this might work, beginning with an elementary classroom.

Activity: Introduce the concepts of addition and subtraction through story problems that students can act out or illustrate.

Benefit: This helps young learners visualize mathematical operations as concrete actions, facilitating a foundational understanding of and personal connection to mathematical procedures.

In a middle school classroom, it might go like this.

Activity: Use manipulatives or digital tools to model geometric transformations such as rotations, reflections, and translations.

Benefit: Hands-on and visual experiences with geometry help students understand the properties and effects of these transformations, enhancing their spatial reasoning and their ability to visually represent mathematical concepts.

And high school teachers might encourage students to explore varied forms of expression in the following ways.

Descriptive Explanations

Activity: Encourage students to write or record video explanations of their processes for solving quadratic equations or calculus problems.

Benefit: This practice allows students to articulate complex processes and reasoning in their own words, reinforcing their understanding and their ability to clearly communicate mathematical ideas.

Visual Representations

Activity: Have students create graphs or use graphing technology to explore different functions and their behavior and properties.

Benefit: Graphing provides visual representations of abstract algebraic concepts, making the relationships and implications of functions clearer and more tangible.

Translational Practice

Activity: Have students translate scenarios into statistical models or use real data to create charts and graphs for presentations.

Benefit: Converting real-world scenarios into mathematical models or statistical representations sharpens students' ability to apply mathematics in practical contexts and enhances their analytical skills.

Intermodal Translation

Activity: Have students convert chemical reaction rates or physics equations into graphs to analyze and predict behaviors.

Benefit: This interdisciplinary application fosters deeper understanding of how mathematical concepts underpin scientific disciplines, enhancing students' overall academic fluency.

By integrating these varied strategies across the K–12 spectrum, teachers can cultivate a dynamic and inclusive learning environment where students are encouraged to engage with mathematical concepts through diverse formats. This approach not only caters to different learning styles but also builds a robust foundation of understanding, making mathematics more accessible and engaging. As students learn to articulate and visualize mathematical concepts in ways that resonate with them, they gain confidence and enthusiasm for exploring and enjoying the subject more deeply.

John Sweller's (2011) research on cognitive load theory emphasizes that reducing extraneous cognitive load and allowing students to focus on core concepts can improve comprehension. By giving students opportunities to represent mathematical ideas through multiple modalities, teachers help them process and internalize complex concepts more efficiently. This aligns with the science of mathematics' emphasis on structured, explicit instruction to optimize learning and problem solving (Fuchs, Newman-Gonchar, et al., 2021; Kong et al., 2021; Powell et al., 2020).

Furthermore, research by Asha K. Jitendra, Gena Nelson, Sandra M. Pulles, Allyson J. Kiss, and James Houseworth (2016) highlights that interventions involving multiple representational formats—such as visual aids alongside procedural practice—are particularly effective for students with learning difficulties. These strategies make mathematics more accessible as well as help students develop a deeper conceptual understanding by allowing them to make connections between different ways of representing a problem.

Additionally, James J. Kaput (1998) underscores the importance of representational fluency, where students who can translate between different mathematical representations (such as graphs, equations, and diagrams) tend to perform better on problem-solving tasks. By encouraging students to articulate and visualize mathematical concepts in ways that resonate with them, teachers foster a more flexible understanding of mathematics, building both competence and confidence.

As students gain confidence in expressing their understanding through various formats, they become more enthusiastic about exploring mathematical concepts. The use of varied strategies not only helps students grasp the subject more deeply but also motivates them to approach problems with a greater sense of curiosity and persistence. Ultimately, this approach fosters a more inclusive and engaging classroom where every student feels empowered to succeed.

Develop Critical Listening and Peer Review

Encouraging students to actively participate by presenting their mathematical ideas and engaging in peer-review sessions is an effective strategy to enhance their communication and critical listening skills. This collaborative approach has students share their own mathematical solutions and interpretations in front of their peers, followed by a constructive critique and discussion session. This dynamic both promotes a deeper understanding of the subject matter and fosters a supportive learning environment where students can refine their reasoning and presentation skills. The following examples describe what this might look like, beginning with an elementary school classroom.

Activity: Conduct math talk circles where students explain their methods for solving simple arithmetic problems or geometric constructions to their peers.

Benefit: Young students begin to learn how to articulate their mathematical thinking and receive immediate feedback. This practice encourages them to think about mathematics communicatively, and it supports their ability to listen to and understand different mathematical approaches.

Similarly, in a middle school classroom, the approach might look like the following.

Activity: Implement structured debates where groups of students argue for different problem-solving strategies, such as the best method to solve a proportion problem or algebraic equation.

Benefit: Middle school students enhance their ability to logically and respectfully argue, critically evaluate different mathematical approaches, and clearly articulate their reasoning. This also helps them appreciate diverse perspectives and develop a deeper understanding of mathematical concepts.

And in high school, it might look like this.

Activity: Organize peer-review sessions where students present their solutions to complex problems or projects, such as statistical analyses or calculus problems, and receive critiques based on clarity, accuracy, and logic.

Benefit: High school students practice delivering detailed explanations and justifications, which prepares them for higher academic pursuits or real-world scenarios where clear and precise communication is crucial. Peer reviews encourage students to critically evaluate their own and others' work, fostering a culture of constructive feedback and continuous improvement.

Broad benefits of this strategy include the following.

- **Improved communication:** By regularly presenting and defending their ideas, students become more adept at structuring their thoughts and communicating them. Jo Boaler (2016) emphasizes that classroom discussions in which students articulate their mathematical thinking help develop communication skills. This process enables students to clarify their reasoning, which makes abstract concepts more concrete and improves their overall ability to explain complex ideas. Studies have also shown that when students are tasked with presenting their solutions and justifying their methods, they become more confident in both written and verbal expression (National Research Council, 2005).

- **Enhanced listening skills:** As students evaluate their peers' explanations, they develop critical listening skills, enhancing their ability to accurately process and understand complex information. Research by Noreen M. Webb (2009) indicates that peer interactions and collaborative problem-solving tasks promote critical listening, as students must pay close attention to the reasoning of others to ask relevant questions and build on their peers' ideas. This fosters an environment of active listening, where students are engaged not just in solving problems but in understanding the diverse approaches their classmates use.

- **Constructive criticism:** Giving and receiving feedback constructively is a valuable life skill that extends beyond the classroom, applicable in both academic and professional settings. John Hattie and Helen Timperley (2007) highlight that feedback is most effective when it is specific, actionable, and received in a supportive environment. Encouraging students to offer constructive criticism to their peers helps them develop the ability to critique ideas, not individuals, and to view feedback as an opportunity for growth. This process builds resilience and prepares students for real-world scenarios where collaboration and feedback are critical for success.

By integrating these practices into the mathematics curriculum, educators can help students enhance their mathematical abilities and also develop essential communication and interpersonal skills. This approach prepares students to engage in thoughtful discourse and to approach mathematical problems with an open and analytical mindset, essential for success in academics and beyond.

Promote Mathematical Discussion

Creating an educational environment that fosters robust mathematical discussions is crucial for developing students' communication skills and their ability to represent mathematical ideas. Such discussions should extend beyond solving problems to include theorizing, exploring mathematical concepts, and interpreting diverse mathematical results. When students engage in detailed discussions, they learn to clearly articulate their mathematical thinking and listen to and integrate the insights of others, enhancing their overall mathematical comprehension. Mathematical discussions can work well in elementary classrooms.

Activity: Implement mathematics explanation sessions where students are tasked with explaining their solutions to class problems using a variety of representations, such as drawings, physical models, and verbal descriptions. Begin with basic arithmetic operations, and encourage students to connect their explanations to visual aids.

Benefit: This encourages young learners to verbalize and visualize mathematical concepts, which fosters a dual development of communication and representational skills. It helps students see the connections between abstract numbers and tangible objects or diagrams, reinforcing their conceptual understanding and ability to communicate these concepts.

In a middle school classroom, mathematical discussion might look like the following.

Activity: Conduct mathematical strategy shares where students present different approaches to solving the same problem, such as finding the area of a complex figure or solving an equation. Each student or group could use a different method or representation, such as algebraic manipulation, geometric visualization, or a digital tool.

Benefit: These sessions enable students to appreciate various problem-solving strategies and understand the effectiveness of different representations. They also learn how to articulate their mathematical processes and justify their choices, which is essential for developing logical reasoning and persuasive communication skills.

And in high school, it might look like this.

Activity: Organize mathematical theory forums where students discuss and critique the application of mathematical theories in real-world contexts, such as in economics, engineering, or environmental science. Encourage them to use and translate between symbolic, numerical, and graphical representations to support their arguments.

Benefit: This helps students link abstract mathematical concepts to practical applications, enhancing their ability to clearly communicate complex ideas. Discussions that require translating between different forms of mathematical expression refine students' ability to think flexibly and present information in the most effective format for their audience.

Benefits of promoting mathematical discussion are well documented through research. Powell and colleagues' (2020) research demonstrates the following advantages.

- **Deepened understanding through representation:** Research by Rittle-Johnson and Schneider (2015) shows that when students discuss different ways to represent mathematical problems and solutions, their understanding of the material deepens. These findings indicate that representations serve not just as solutions but as explanations that facilitate clearer communication about abstract concepts, leading to improved mathematical comprehension.

- **Enhanced communication through discussion:** According to Hwang and Riccomini (2016), regular discussion of mathematical ideas significantly improves students' verbal and written communication skills. Their research demonstrates that mathematical discourse teaches students to clearly express complex thoughts and listen to others' perspectives, critical skills in any academic or professional field.

- **Integrated learning experience:** A study by Morgan and colleagues (2015) shows that combining communication and representation in discussions makes learning more integrative and less segmented. This research indicates that students who engage in such integrated discussions see mathematics as a dynamic field that involves explaining, representing, and understanding, not just computing, leading to better overall mathematical achievement.

By incorporating these structured discussion activities into the mathematics curriculum, educators empower students to master both the content of mathematics and the skills necessary to effectively communicate and represent mathematical ideas. This holistic approach makes students not only better mathematicians but also more articulate and thoughtful individuals.

Conclusion

In this chapter, we have explored the pivotal roles of communication and representation within the CMC framework, emphasizing their crucial impact on fostering deep mathematical understanding and expression. As we've seen, this competency does more than facilitate the mere transmission of mathematical ideas; it transforms how students perceive, interact with, and express these ideas, turning abstract concepts into tangible and manipulable realities.

As students develop their abilities to communicate and represent mathematical ideas, they also build critical bridges between theoretical knowledge and practical application. This skill set is indispensable in academic settings and in everyday problem-solving and decision-making scenarios they will encounter outside the classroom. By equipping students with this competency, educators are not just teaching mathematics; they are instilling a capacity for analytical thinking, problem solving, and creativity that students will carry with them into all areas of their lives.

Thus, communication and representation stand not merely as elements to be taught but as foundational practices that weave throughout the entire fabric of mathematics education, enhancing every other competency of mathematical proficiency. As educators continue to nurture this competency, they contribute to a robust, dynamic, and deeply engaged mathematical culture in their classrooms—one where every student has the tools to understand mathematics and to actively contribute to it.

CHAPTER 6

Strategic Use of Tools and Precision

As we delve deeper into the CMC framework, focus turns to the strategic use of tools and precision. This competency underscores the critical role of mathematical tools and precision in shaping students' expertise in mathematics and how this understanding progresses in later grades.

The paradigm shift in how algebra is taught in schools vividly illustrates the transformative impact of strategic tool use and precision in mathematics education (Fey & Phillips, 2009). Research by Powell and colleagues (2020) demonstrates that this shift has been characterized by an increased emphasis on understanding patterns, functions, and variations—a focus that is ideally introduced in elementary grades and developed through middle school.

In this evolving landscape, the judicious selection and application of mathematical tools—ranging from basic calculators to advanced software capable of handling complex algebraic manipulations and graphical representations—plays a pivotal role. These tools do not merely facilitate computational tasks; they extend the range and depth of mathematical concepts that students can explore and understand. For instance, graphing calculators and dynamic geometry software enable students to visualize complex functions and geometric transformations with much greater ease and accuracy than traditional methods. Studies by Christian T. Doabler and colleagues (2015) and Paul Drijvers,

Aad Goddijn, and Martin Kindt (2011) show that strategic integration of mathematical tools significantly improves students' conceptual understanding and problem-solving capabilities. This finding is further supported by Hughes and colleagues (2017), whose research demonstrates that effective use of technological tools, when combined with explicit instruction, enhances students' mathematical proficiency and problem-solving skills.

Moreover, the strategic use of these tools is complemented by a rigorous approach to precision in mathematical reasoning and expression. Precision is not just about getting the right answer; it involves meticulously approaching the process of mathematical thinking, from correctly setting out problems to accurately interpreting results. This attention to detail ensures that students perform calculations correctly as well as understand the underlying principles and can apply them in varied contexts.

For example, in a high school algebra class, students might use graphing tools to explore the behavior of quadratic functions. By manipulating the coefficients and observing the changes in the graphs, students gain a deeper understanding of the relationship between algebraic expressions and their graphical representations. This hands-on approach, supported by precise tools and clear instructions, helps solidify their understanding of key algebraic concepts such as vertex form, intercepts, and symmetry.

The strategic use of tools and a focus on precision also encourage students to consider the implications of their mathematical decisions. When working on a problem, students learn to ask critical questions: Which tool is most appropriate for this task? What level of precision is required in the calculation? How will the choice of tool and the level of precision affect the outcome? Engaging with these questions enhances their analytical skills and fosters a mindset that values careful consideration and thoroughness.

Thus, the strategic use of tools and precision not only enhances students' ability to handle complex mathematical tasks but also cultivates a more nuanced understanding of mathematics. This chapter will explore various strategies and instructional practices that promote this competency, providing students with the skills and knowledge necessary to excel in mathematics and beyond.

The Essence of Strategic Use of Tools and Precision

The strategic use of tools involves selecting the most appropriate mathematical instruments—be they calculators, software, or manipulatives—to effectively tackle specific problems. Precision in mathematics goes beyond mere accuracy of calculation; it encompasses clarity of thought, exactness of expression, and rigor in argumentation. In other words, this competency requires choosing and utilizing appropriate mathematical tools that not only streamline calculations but also increase the accuracy and efficiency of mathematical tasks. Such strategic choices enable students to engage more deeply with analytical tasks and complex problem solving, freeing them from the burdens of tedious computation. This chapter will explore how the judicious application of tools—ranging from traditional manipulatives to advanced digital technologies—can transform students' learning experiences in mathematical endeavors.

Selecting the right tools for mathematical tasks is critical in improving both the accuracy and the efficiency of student work. Research by Fuchs, Newman-Gonchar, and colleagues (2021) demonstrates that when students use appropriate tools for computation, data visualization, or geometric construction, they show significant improvements in accuracy and completion speed. This finding is reinforced by Amanda M. VanDerHeyden and Robin Codding (2020), whose work shows that strategic tool selection reduces error rates and increases computational efficiency. Moreover, Stevens and colleagues (2018) find through their meta-analysis that students who have access to and training in appropriate mathematical tools demonstrate higher levels of mathematical proficiency and make fewer computational errors compared to those who lack such resources. This precision both fosters confidence and allows students to allocate more mental resources to understanding underlying concepts and solving more complex problems.

By enhancing the accuracy and efficiency of mathematical tasks, tools not only improve students' performance but also deepen their engagement with the material in the following ways.

- **Precision in calculations:** Tools like scientific calculators, graphing calculators, and computational software can perform complex arithmetic and algebraic operations with high accuracy. This precision is crucial when taking examinations or solving real-world problems where exact calculations are necessary.

- **Efficient problem solving:** Software tools that automate routine procedures, such as solving equations or graphing functions, save time and reduce cognitive load. This efficiency enables students to concentrate on strategy development and deeper understanding of the problem at hand rather than on the mechanics of calculation.

- **Visual accuracy in geometry:** Digital tools like dynamic geometry software provide precise visual representations of geometric concepts, which are essential for understanding properties of shapes, proving geometric theorems, and solving construction problems. These tools ensure that students can experiment with and visualize complex geometric relationships without the inaccuracies that often come with manual drawing.

- **Data handling and analysis:** Statistical software and apps that facilitate data analysis allow students to manage large datasets efficiently and accurately. They can easily compute statistical measures, create graphs, and interpret data patterns, which are critical skills in many fields of study and sectors of employment.

- **Enhanced learning through simulation:** Simulations provide a way to explore mathematical models and theories through interactive environments. They help students understand dynamic systems and complex variable interactions with greater precision and less effort compared to traditional methods.

As students become adept at using these tools, they develop a keener sense of when and how to apply different technologies to various mathematical challenges, thus honing their judgment and problem-solving skills. This strategic competence is essential for academic success in mathematics and is invaluable in many professional fields where precision and efficiency are prized. Teachers would do well to explore the many opportunities that digital tools offer as well as to examine the interplay of strategic tool use with other competencies in the CMC framework.

Digital Tools

The strategic use of digital tools can significantly enhance the learning experience by offering interactive, visual, and intuitive ways to explore complex mathematical concepts. These tools provide dynamic environments where students can manipulate elements, visualize abstract concepts, and receive immediate feedback on their actions, making them indispensable for modern classrooms.

Here are some examples of digital tools and their benefits.

- **Fraction representation tools (apps like circle and bar models):** These apps help students visualize fractions with denominators from 1 to 100, allowing them to see the relationships and operations of fractions in a more concrete way. By manipulating these visual models, students can develop a deeper understanding of fraction concepts, equivalent fractions, and fraction operations.
- **Virtual geoboards:** Stretching virtual bands around pegs to form line segments and polygons aids in the study of geometry and enhances understanding of concepts like perimeter and area. These tools are particularly effective for hands-on learning and experimentation with geometric shapes.

- **Interactive clock apps:** Exploring time, fractions, and other numerical concepts through virtual clocks with geared or free-moving hands can make abstract concepts like time measurement more tangible. These tools are excellent for integrating real-life applications of mathematics in classroom discussions.

- **Digital vocabulary cards:** These apps deepen understanding of key mathematical terms through written and visual definitions, supporting vocabulary development and conceptual understanding across various mathematical topics.

- **Virtual money manipulatives:** These tools allow students to visualize and understand money values and their relationships using currency simulations. They're particularly useful for practical mathematics and financial literacy education.

- **Interactive number charts:** These apps allow for the exploration of number patterns or the creation of grids that can include fractions, decimals, and more; they foster an environment where numerical relationships can be visually investigated and understood.

- **Digital number frames:** By placing counters inside frames of various sizes, students can visually represent numbers. This cultivates number sense and an understanding of the base-ten system, and is particularly effective for young learners beginning to explore numbers.

- **Number line apps:** These dynamic tools allow students to visualize and manipulate number sequences, mathematical operations, and relationships on a customizable number line. Students can zoom in to explore decimal places or out to view larger numbers, making these apps particularly useful for understanding number magnitude and operations across different numerical ranges.

- **Virtual number lines:** These tools provide linear representations of numbers, which can be used to teach addition, subtraction, and number sequences. Adjustable

Strategic Use of Tools and Precision

features like tick marks enhance customization to suit different teaching objectives.

- **Number pieces:** These digital manipulatives allow students to work with individual units and groupings, helping them understand place value, regrouping, and basic arithmetic operations. Students can break apart and combine these virtual pieces to explore number relationships and develop number sense.
- **Virtual base-ten blocks:** These digital blocks help students understand multidigit numbers, place value, and basic operations by allowing them to manipulate virtual pieces that represent ones, tens, and hundreds.
- **Number rack:** A virtual version of the traditional arithmetic rack, this tool displays two rows of beads that students can slide to visualize quantities and develop mental mathematics strategies. It's especially effective for building early number sense and understanding combinations of numbers up to 20.
- **Bead-sliding tool:** Similar to an abacus, this digital tool helps students visualize number relationships and basic arithmetic by sliding bead groupings of fives and tens.
- **Partial product finder:** This interactive tool helps students understand the distributive property and the partial product method of multiplication. Students can break down larger multiplication problems into smaller, more manageable parts, visualizing how the partial products combine to create the final product.
- **Multiplication visualization:** This tool helps students understand the area model of multiplication by allowing them to create rectangles or arrays that visually represent multiplication combinations.
- **Virtual pattern blocks:** Students can explore counting, geometry, fractions, and more with these digital blocks, which make abstract concepts like symmetry or tessellation more accessible and engaging.

In the strategic use of tools and precision within the CMC framework, integrating technology is key. The thoughtful selection of digital tools not only boosts computational accuracy but also reinforces other competency elements, such as conceptual understanding and problem solving. Leveraging these tools facilitates a more nuanced approach to mathematics, empowering students to explore, model, and visualize mathematical concepts in innovative ways.

Following are several tech tools designed to foster precision in mathematical calculations and problem solving. These digital tools, which are free or offer robust free versions suitable for educational use, ensure accessibility while enhancing precision in mathematics education across different grade levels.

- **Desmos (www.desmos.com):** This powerful online graphing calculator is invaluable for visualizing algebraic equations, exploring transformations, and understanding functions. Desmos supports a wide range of activities that integrate other competency elements such as problem solving, making it a versatile tool in the mathematics classroom.

- **GeoGebra (www.geogebra.org):** GeoGebra offers dynamic mathematics software that combines geometry, algebra, and calculus tools. It is perfect for creating constructions and modeling situations that require a precise understanding of mathematical relationships, and thereby enhances conceptual and procedural integration.

- **Khan Academy (www.khanacademy.org):** This platform provides a vast range of instructional videos and practice exercises that cover every major mathematics topic. It is excellent for reinforcing concepts and enhancing precision and conceptual understanding.

- **PhET Interactive Simulations (https://phet.colorado.edu):** Hosted by the University of Colorado Boulder, PhET offers free interactive mathematics and science simulations. These tools help students visualize abstract concepts, directly engaging them in an interactive learning process that promotes both understanding and accuracy.

- **CK–12 Foundation (www.ck12.org/student):** CK–12 provides a comprehensive set of free online textbooks and resources for students and teachers. It offers customizable content and interactive lessons, particularly useful in aligning with the conceptual understanding and problem-solving elements of the CMC framework.

- **Microsoft Math Solver (https://math.microsoft.com):** This app includes tools that help with solving mathematical problems and visualizing concepts in new and intuitive ways. Its graphing calculator gives a visual representation of mathematical functions, enhancing students' understanding of the material.

- **Mathway (www.mathway.com):** While there is a premium version, Mathway's free features let students solve problems across a range of topics from basic arithmetic to higher mathematics. It helps students develop problem-solving skills by providing step-by-step solutions and demonstrating precise mathematical techniques.

- **Number Line by Brainingcamp (www.brainingcamp.com/number-lines):** This tool helps students visualize number sequences and demonstrate strategies for counting, comparing, and arithmetic. It's particularly effective in illustrating conceptual mathematics in a clear and precise manner.

- **WolframAlpha (www.wolframalpha.com):** Known for its computational intelligence and AI capabilities, this answer engine allows students to solve complex calculations and explore step-by-step solutions, aiding them in the development of logical reasoning and procedural fluency. Teachers should guide students to do the following.

- Use WolframAlpha to verify solutions after attempting problems.
- Analyze the step-by-step explanations to deepen understanding.
- Compare different solution methods.

- **ChatGPT, Claude, Microsoft Copilot, and similar large language model tools:** While these tools can perform mathematical operations quickly, they should be strategically used to do the following.
  - Check work and explore alternative solution methods.
  - Analyze mathematical reasoning and problem-solving approaches.
  - Practice explaining mathematical concepts.

Note: Teachers should emphasize understanding over automation and help students develop critical evaluation skills when using AI tools.

By incorporating these digital resources, teachers can provide students with the means to deeply understand and accurately apply mathematical concepts. These tools support precision and foster an environment where students can experiment and solve problems more effectively, thus preparing them for advanced studies and professional fields where mathematical precision is paramount.

To effectively integrate these digital tools into your teaching, consider the following strategies.

- **Direct integration:** Use the tools during lessons to demonstrate new concepts or solve problems together as a class.
- **Individual exploration:** Allow students time to explore these tools independently or in small groups to solve specific tasks or challenges.
- **Assessment and feedback:** Utilize these tools for assessments where students can demonstrate their understanding in a digital format, and provide instant feedback.

- **Flipped classroom:** Assign interactive activities as homework to prepare students for more in-depth discussion and problem solving in class.
- **Blended learning:** Combine traditional teaching methods with these digital tools to cater to various learning styles and needs.

By carefully selecting and utilizing these digital tools, you can provide a rich, engaging, and effective mathematical learning experience that builds foundational skills and also prepares students for the technological demands of the future. These tools are not just supplementary; they are transformative elements that can significantly enhance the precision and understanding of mathematical concepts among students.

Interplay Between Tool Use and Other Competencies

The adoption of concrete tools, often referred to as manipulatives, has become a foundational practice in teaching mathematics, especially at the elementary level. It's essential to recognize that manipulatives serve as facilitative tools rather than final objectives. Their effective utilization requires a thoughtful approach, knowing when, why, and how to use them to enhance mathematics learning and giving students ample time to explore these tools to develop meaningful understanding and establish connections between concepts.

The strategic use of tools, particularly manipulatives, demonstrates the interconnected nature of the CMC framework's competencies. Deployment of these tools can transform abstract mathematical ideas into accessible, interactive experiences that enhance student engagement and understanding. For instance, stacking or removing base-ten blocks can help students visualize the process of addition or subtraction. Similarly, fraction tiles provide a clear visual representation of how fractions combine and relate to each other.

While chapter 5 (page 95) addresses how physical representations support mathematical understanding, here we explore how strategic tool use enhances and integrates with other competencies. Research by Powell and colleagues (2020) demonstrates that effective tool use strengthens multiple aspects of mathematics learning simultaneously.

According to Morgan and colleagues (2015), the thoughtful deployment of manipulatives strengthens students' ability to communicate mathematical ideas and represent concepts in multiple ways, such as the following.

- Base-ten blocks enable students to demonstrate and explain regrouping processes to peers, combining tool use with mathematical communication.
- Fraction tiles allow students to physically represent and discuss part-to-whole relationships, supporting both precise tool use and mathematical discourse.
- Geometric manipulatives help students explain spatial relationships while developing precise measurement skills.

When it comes to conceptual and procedural integration (chapter 2, page 25), studies by Rittle-Johnson (2017) show that manipulatives serve as a bridge between conceptual understanding and procedural fluency when used strategically, such as in the following examples.

- Students use Cuisenaire rods to explore number relationships before learning formal arithmetic procedures.
- Algebra tiles help students connect concrete modeling to abstract algebraic manipulation.
- Logic blocks support the progression from physical sorting to abstract classification skills.

As for the competency of problem solving and modeling (chapter 3, page 47), research by Hwang and Riccomini (2016) demonstrates how strategic tool use directly supports problem-solving capabilities, like in the following examples.

- Students use chips for operational trading to model and solve word problems.

Strategic Use of Tools and Precision

- Unifix cubes help students visualize and solve measurement problems.
- Pattern blocks enable exploration of geometric problem-solving strategies.

To maximize these connections, Doabler and colleagues (2015) recommend that teachers employ the following actions.

- Choose tools purposefully.
  - Select manipulatives that support both conceptual understanding and procedural development.
  - Ensure tools can be used for both problem exploration and precise calculation.
  - Consider how tools can support mathematical communication.
- Guide strategic progression.
  - Begin with concrete exploration.
  - Move to representational drawings.
  - Transition to abstract symbols.
  - Maintain connections between all representations.
- Support precise use.
  - Model accurate tool use.
  - Encourage precise mathematical language.
  - Connect physical actions to mathematical principles.

By carefully integrating manipulatives into the mathematics curriculum and aligning their use with clear educational goals, teachers can significantly enhance students' understanding and enjoyment of mathematics. Doing so with precision is crucial. Educators must guide students not just to manipulate objects but to reflect on their actions and articulate the mathematical principles they are exploring. This reflection helps deepen their comprehension and cements the connection between the physical activity and the abstract mathematical ideas it represents.

Strategically incorporating these tools in the curriculum ensures that students not only perform mathematical operations but also understand the underlying concepts, and thus build a solid foundation for more advanced mathematics learning. This approach aligns with the broader goals of the CMC framework, emphasizing the importance of precise, thoughtful engagement with mathematical tools to foster a more comprehensive understanding of mathematics from an early age.

Strategies to Enhance Strategic Use of Tools and Precision

Enhancing the strategic use of tools and precision in the classroom involves cultivating students' ability to articulate and solve problems with clear, exact language and symbols. Research by Powell and colleagues (2020) demonstrates that when tools and precision are systematically integrated, students develop stronger mathematical understanding and problem-solving capabilities. The strategic use of tools and precision in mathematics requires thoughtful implementation across grade levels. This systematic approach must be carefully scaffolded to match students' developmental readiness while progressively building their capacity for tool use and precision.

The selection and implementation of mathematical tools should follow a clear progression that aligns with students' mathematical development. At the elementary level, students begin their journey with basic technological tools that support fundamental mathematical understanding. Teachers introduce basic calculators to support arithmetic operations, ensuring students first develop strong mental mathematics and estimation skills. Simple graphing platforms like Desmos can be used to create basic visualizations, helping students understand number patterns and relationships. Digital manipulatives serve as virtual counterparts to physical tools, allowing students to explore mathematical concepts in an interactive environment. For example, first-grade students might use digital number lines to visualize addition and subtraction, which builds both tool proficiency and numerical understanding. By third grade, students can transition to using calculators strategically, such as verifying computations after solving problems manually.

As students progress to middle school, they encounter more sophisticated tools that support deeper mathematical exploration. Scientific calculators and geometry software become essential tools for investigating more complex mathematical relationships. GeoGebra and similar platforms enable students to dynamically explore geometric concepts, while data-analysis tools help them understand statistical concepts through hands-on investigation. For instance, seventh-grade students might use GeoGebra to investigate angle relationships, measuring and constructing geometric figures with precision. Projects at this level often integrate multiple tools to solve real-world problems involving area, perimeter, and statistical analysis; this way, students understand how different tools can work together to support problem solving.

High school students transition to professional-grade tools that prepare them for advanced academic work and future careers. These tools support sophisticated modeling and analysis applications, allowing students to tackle complex mathematical challenges. Students learn to effectively combine multiple tools, using platforms like Desmos alongside spreadsheet software to analyze real-world data and create mathematical models. Advanced courses incorporate specialized software for statistical analysis and calculus concepts to help students develop proficiency with tools they'll encounter in college and professional settings.

Successful implementation of these tools requires careful attention to several key considerations. Teachers must ensure regular training and updates for both themselves and their students to keep pace with evolving technology. Rather than treating tools as additions to the curriculum, teachers should integrate them into daily instruction so they become natural extensions of mathematical thinking and problem solving. Students need explicit instruction in understanding when and why to use specific tools so they develop critical thinking skills about tool selection. This thoughtful approach to implementation helps students

Precision in Problem Statements

One effective method to underscore the importance of clarity in mathematics is to present students with intentionally vague or ambiguously worded problem statements. Encourage students to identify areas lacking clarity and rewrite the problems to ensure precision and understandability before attempting to solve them. This task pushes students to consider what information is essential for making these problems solvable and to articulate the problems in a clear, structured way. Precision is indispensable in mathematics, where small discrepancies or unclear reasoning can fundamentally skew conclusions. Ensuring precision helps students articulate and justify their mathematical reasoning with clarity, which fosters robust understanding and effective communication.

The following examples describe how teachers can instill a culture of precision in mathematics classrooms across different instructional levels, beginning with elementary school.

Activity: Use precise language and specific instructions when teaching basic arithmetic operations. For example, when introducing subtraction, clarify terms like *minuend*, *subtrahend*, and *difference*, and demonstrate how each part of the subtraction equation relates to these terms.

Implementation: During mathematics lessons, encourage students to verbalize their thought processes step by step as they solve problems, correcting and refining their language and calculations in real time. This practice not only helps them deeply understand operations but also teaches them the importance of using the correct mathematical vocabulary and procedures.

Benefit: Young learners begin to appreciate the importance of precision early on, which helps prevent misconceptions that could complicate learning more complex mathematical concepts later.

Strategic Use of Tools and Precision

Middle school teachers might incorporate precision in the following way.

Activity: Introduce activities that require precise measurement and data handling, such as geometry projects where students must accurately use rulers and protractors to construct and measure angles and sides of shapes.

Implementation: Conduct regular peer-review sessions where students present their mathematical solutions and receive feedback on the precision of their reasoning and calculations. Students could check each other's work for errors in logic or calculation, discuss alternative solutions, and refine their presentations.

Benefit: Students develop a keen eye for detail and learn to constructively critique mathematical arguments. This not only enhances their understanding but also prepares them for high-stakes testing and advanced study, where precision is crucial.

High school teachers could use an activity such as the following.

Activity: Engage students in higher-level mathematics, such as calculus or statistics, where precision is critical for solving problems involving limits, derivatives, or data interpretation.

Implementation: Utilize technology like graphing calculators or software to allow students to explore and visualize complex mathematical concepts. For example, in statistics, students might use software to precisely calculate and interpret standard deviations and correlation coefficients.

Benefit: High school students learn to handle abstract concepts with accuracy and develop skills necessary for scientific and quantitative reasoning in higher education and professional fields.

Teachers throughout K–12 can keep the following items in mind.

- **Consistent feedback:** Incorporate ongoing assessments that focus not just on the correct answers but on the methods used to arrive at those answers. Provide detailed feedback on students' calculation processes and reasoning, highlighting areas where precision is lacking.

- **Mathematical discussions:** Foster an environment where mathematical discussion is routine. Encourage students to articulate their reasoning during these discussions, and challenge them to justify their answers with clear, logical explanations.

- **Modeling of precision:** Model precision in your own explanations and use of mathematical language. This modeling shows students the importance of accuracy in mathematical communication and computation.

By embedding these practices across all levels of education, teachers can create a robust mathematical foundation for students. This foundation improves students' problem-solving skills and prepares them for future academic and career challenges that require mathematical precision. This systematic focus on precision in problem statements serves to deepen students' understanding of the problem-solving process itself, enhancing their ability to dissect and tackle complex problems systematically.

Symbol Usage Workshops

Regularly scheduled workshops focused on the correct use and interpretation of mathematical symbols can significantly enhance students' understanding and prevent common errors. Such sessions can explore the proper use of symbols like equals signs, square roots, and function notations, discussing their meanings and common misconceptions. These workshops help students recognize the potential for miscommunication in mathematics and appreciate the precision required for effective mathematical discourse. This deep dive into symbolic language not only prevents computational errors but also enriches students' capacity to engage with advanced mathematical concepts.

Peer Review of Mathematical Writing

Incorporating peer-review sessions where students exchange written explanations of their problem-solving processes can be tremendously beneficial. In these sessions, students critique each other's use of mathematical language and the logical flow of their solutions. This activity prompts students to more clearly and precisely express complex ideas as well as enhances their critical evaluation skills. Reviewing a peer's work provides a dual benefit: It reinforces the reviewer's understanding of the subject matter and refines their ability to effectively communicate mathematical ideas. Furthermore, it cultivates a classroom culture where precision and clarity are valued and upheld by all members, promoting a collaborative and supportive learning environment.

Modeling and Fostering of Meticulous Problem-Solving Techniques

The ability to apply tools strategically and execute mathematical procedures precisely is not merely about achieving correct answers; it's about cultivating a meticulous approach to mathematical thinking. This focus on exactness and careful analysis is crucial for developing students' competence in handling complex mathematical concepts accurately and confidently across all grade levels. By embedding meticulous problem-solving techniques into daily teaching practices, educators can significantly boost students' mathematical skills, ensuring they are capable of solving problems with efficiency and adept at communicating and justifying their mathematical reasoning with clarity and precision.

The following actionable examples and techniques can be tailored to fit the learning needs of students from elementary to high school, fostering a robust mathematical foundation grounded in careful thought and precision. For elementary school, consider the following.

> **Activity:** Use a problem-solving checklist for simple arithmetic problems, such as addition or subtraction. After solving a problem, students should check their answers by applying the inverse operation. For instance, if they have calculated 8 + 7 = 15, they can subtract 7 from 15 to ensure the result is 8.
>
> **Benefit:** This strategy encourages students to independently verify their results, reinforcing their understanding of inverse operations and instilling a habit of accuracy and self-correction. It also helps young learners build confidence in their calculations and reduce careless errors.

For middle school, consider the following.

Activity: Implement a structured approach to solving algebraic expressions by breaking them into parts. For instance, in a problem like $2x + 5 = 15$, students should first isolate the term with the variable by subtracting 5 from both sides to get $2x = 10$ and then divide by 2 to solve for x. Encourage students to write each step clearly and check each phase of their solution for possible errors.

Benefit: This step-by-step approach helps students manage their work without feeling overwhelmed, especially when dealing with variables and equations for the first time. It enhances students' problem-solving skills and ensures they understand the logical progression of algebraic manipulations, which prepares them for more complex algebraic problems.

And for high school, consider the following.

Activity: Instruct students in the meticulous application of algebraic methods to solve quadratic equations using the quadratic formula. For example, with the equation $x^2 - 5x + 6 = 0$, students would first identify coefficients and then apply the quadratic formula $\frac{-b \pm \sqrt{b^2 - 4ac}}{2a}$. Encourage students to detail each step, including simplifying the discriminant, calculating the square root, and performing the final operations to find x.

Benefit: Requiring high school students to document each step in solving algebraic equations helps them learn to be methodical and precise. This minimizes computational errors and also improves understanding of the underlying concepts. Detailed documentation makes it easier for students to review their work and understand where they might have gone wrong, which is crucial for their success in higher-level mathematics.

By integrating these strategies, you can foster a mathematical environment that emphasizes and rewards precision in both language and thought. This preparation is crucial, not only for academic success but also for real-world applications.

Conclusion

This chapter's exploration within the CMC framework has underscored the pivotal role of strategic use of tools and precision in mathematics education. This competency is essential not just for fostering accurate and efficient mathematical practice but also for cultivating a deep, nuanced understanding of mathematical concepts. Through the strategic use of tools, students are equipped with the means to explore and manipulate mathematical ideas in a way that abstract pencil-and-paper methods alone cannot achieve. Precision in their approach and communication further ensures that these explorations yield clear, correct, and transferable knowledge.

The integration of modern digital tools, from dynamic geometry software to advanced graphing calculators, exemplifies how technology can enhance learning experiences, offering students both the visibility and the flexibility needed to tackle complex mathematical problems. These tools do not merely serve to simplify calculations; they act as bridges connecting theoretical concepts with real-world applications, thereby enriching the learning process and preparing students for the technological and mathematical demands of the future. Moreover, the meticulous nature of mathematical language and symbols, which I have emphasized throughout this chapter, is crucial in nurturing students who are mathematically literate as well as precise and articulate in their reasoning. This precision is not an end in itself but a means to achieving clarity of thought and depth of understanding.

Incorporating manipulatives into the curriculum enhances this precision and understanding, providing tangible, hands-on experiences that make abstract concepts more accessible and engaging. Tools like base-ten blocks, Cuisenaire rods, and fraction tiles help students visualize and physically manipulate mathematical concepts, which reinforces their learning and fosters a deeper connection with the material. These physical tools are complemented by their digital counterparts, which extend the range of exploration and interaction available to students. As we encourage students to employ a variety of tools and uphold precision in their mathematical endeavors, we are also fostering a mindset attuned to detail, a habit of rigorous analysis, and an appreciation for the subtleties of mathematical discourse. These skills are invaluable, transcending the boundaries of mathematics to support thoughtful, analytical engagement with the world.

This chapter, therefore, serves to highlight specific strategies and tools and frame them as integral components of a comprehensive instructional approach. In fostering the strategic use of tools and precision, we prepare students for academic success and for a lifetime of thoughtful problem solving and informed decision making, where precision and strategic thinking are essential.

CHAPTER 7

Structural Insight and Regularity

This chapter explores the profound role of structural insight and regularity within the CMC framework. Algorithms embody more than mere steps to solve problems; they represent conceptual insights that address whole classes of mathematical challenges. This perspective reveals mathematics as a structured, pattern-rich, and predictable discipline, where well-developed procedures transcend simple problem solving to become robust tools for broader application. As educators, we have a pivotal role in guiding students to see beyond the procedural execution to the underlying structures that make these algorithms powerful and universally applicable. Let's take a closer look at the nature of this competency before reviewing practical strategies and insights to help students appreciate and harness structures and patterns for deeper mathematical understanding.

The Essence of Structural Insight and Regularity

Structural insight and regularity are fundamental elements that delve into recognizing and comprehending the patterns and systematic frameworks that underpin mathematical concepts. Research by Schneider and colleagues (2011) demonstrates that this proficiency is crucial for students, as it enables them to move beyond the specifics of isolated problems and comprehend the broader principles that govern entire mathematical systems. Studies synthesized by Powell and colleagues (2020) show that by cultivating this competency, students significantly enhance their ability to engage in sophisticated problem solving and reasoning.

Research has highlighted the importance of pattern recognition and structural insight in mathematics education. According to the National Council of Teachers of Mathematics (2000), "Recognizing and understanding patterns and structure reduces complexity and leads to deeper understanding, allowing predictions and generalizations to be made from less information" (p. 64). This foundational understanding has since been reinforced by further research. Rittle-Johnson (2017) demonstrates that structural insight not only facilitates the learning of new mathematical concepts but also enhances cognitive retention and application. Furthermore, studies by Cook and colleagues (2020) and Sue Johnston-Wilder and John Mason (2005) indicate that students who are trained to recognize mathematical structures develop more flexible and deeper understanding of mathematics, leading to improved problem-solving capabilities across various mathematical domains.

For instance, understanding the pattern behind the sequence of odd numbers enables students to predict subsequent numbers and apply this knowledge to more complex arithmetic operations. Another example can be seen in algebra, where recognizing the structure of a quadratic equation helps students anticipate the shape of its graph and the nature of its roots. In geometry, recognizing the properties of shapes and their relationships can lead to quicker and more accurate problem-solving strategies. For example, understanding that the sum of the internal angles in any triangle is always 180 degrees helps students solve for unknown angles without the need for complex calculations. Further, in the realm of data analysis, recognizing patterns in datasets allows students to effectively make predictions and inferences. For instance, identifying a linear trend in a scatterplot enables predictions about future data points, which is a key skill in statistics.

Thus, the development of structural insight and regularity not only sharpens students' problem-solving skills but also prepares them for higher-level mathematics and various real-world applications. By embedding this competency in the curriculum, educators can provide students with the tools to see beyond surface-level information and to understand the deeper, more universal logic that mathematics offers.

Let's explore more examples of structural insight and regularity. When students recognize that the distributive property underlies the process of expanding expressions like $(a + b)(c + d)$, they gain a tool that applies across a range of algebraic problems, not just single instances. This insight helps them understand why the property works and how it can be used to efficiently simplify and solve more complex equations. Moreover, this competency encourages students to explore and appreciate the beauty and predictability of mathematics. They begin to see patterns in sequences, symmetry in equations, and regularity in geometric figures, which can lead to deeper curiosity about and engagement with the subject. By encouraging students to look for and articulate these structures, educators can foster a mathematical mindset that values rigor and coherence, equipping students with a powerful approach to both academic challenges and real-world scenarios.

In teaching structural insight and regularity, educators can employ strategies such as pattern recognition exercises, explorations of mathematical theorems in geometry, or investigations into functions and their transformations. These activities both solidify students' understanding of mathematical concepts and emphasize the interconnectedness of different areas of mathematics, showing how various concepts align within a coherent framework. Emphasizing structural insight and regularity in the classroom helps students build a robust mathematical foundation, which empowers them to apply these principles to new and unfamiliar problems. This approach both enhances their problem-solving skills and nurtures a profound appreciation for the logical structure and elegance of mathematics. Let's dig a little deeper into the importance of this competency before exploring its interplay with other competencies.

The Importance of Structural Insight and Regularity

Recognizing underlying structures in mathematics significantly deepens students' comprehension of the subject. This competency enables students to grasp not just how mathematical operations are performed but why these operations work. For example, understanding the principles behind the distributive property helps students see how it unifies various algebraic processes, such as expanding brackets and simplifying expressions. This understanding promotes a more cohesive and integrated grasp of mathematics, turning routine procedures into insightful explorations of mathematical logic.

Insight into the inherent structures of mathematical systems enhances students' ability to predict outcomes and properties within these systems. This skill is invaluable in academic settings, where it can facilitate problem solving and hypothesis testing, as well as in real-world scenarios, such as financial forecasting and engineering. For instance, recognizing geometric patterns and symmetries can help students predict the outcomes of physical transformations, such as rotations or reflections, which are crucial in fields like physics and computer graphics.

A deep understanding of the regularities and patterns in mathematics equips students with the foundational knowledge necessary to innovate and adapt known concepts to new challenges. This ability to innovate is particularly important in rapidly evolving fields such as technology and science, where new problems often require novel solutions that build on established mathematical principles. For example, understanding the regularity in number sequences may inspire students to develop new algorithms for data encryption or to solve complex computational problems more efficiently. By fostering an appreciation for and understanding of structural insight and regularity, educators empower students to master mathematics and to apply it creatively and effectively in diverse situations. This approach not only enriches students' mathematics education but also prepares them to contribute to advancing various scientific and technological areas.

A Distinct yet Interwoven Competency

Structural insight and regularity is a distinct competency within the CMC framework that uniquely focuses on recognizing and understanding the patterns and systematic frameworks in mathematics across various contexts. This competency extends beyond the skills honed through logical reasoning, such as following a sequence of steps to arrive at a conclusion or solve a problem; it presents a distinct and separate thread that addresses these patterns and frameworks across various contexts. Logical reasoning is critical for developing arguments and understanding processes within individual scenarios, but structural insight and regularity equips students to recognize and leverage recurring themes and structures across different mathematical contexts. This competency helps students understand how different concepts are interrelated and governed by common principles, which enhances their ability to reason about mathematics in a more generalized and abstract way.

Problem solving is primarily about applying known strategies to find solutions to specific problems. It involves understanding the problem, devising a plan, carrying out that plan, and then looking back to check and extend the results. In contrast, structural insight and regularity is about seeing the bigger picture—identifying the inherent patterns and regularities in mathematics that can simplify and inform the approach to a wide range of problems. This competency encourages students to step back and consider the mathematical landscape more broadly, enabling them to recognize that certain strategies and approaches can be universally applied due to the structured nature of mathematics itself.

For example, in teaching structural insight and regularity, educators might focus on how the properties of operations (like commutativity and associativity) apply across various mathematical systems, from whole numbers to matrices. This helps students see that these properties are not just rules to follow but indicators of deeper structural truths about mathematical operations. In contrast, a logical reasoning lesson might have students prove, through a series of logical steps, why the sum of a triangle's angles is always 180 degrees, while a problem-solving activity might have students apply specific algorithms to calculate the areas of triangles in different contexts.

By distinguishing structural insight and regularity as a separate competency, the CMC framework emphasizes the importance of a foundational understanding that enhances all other areas of mathematics learning, including logical reasoning and problem solving. This not only deepens students' mathematical knowledge but also empowers them with a versatile tool kit that can be adapted to a diverse range of academic and real-world challenges.

Strategies to Enhance Structural Insight and Regularity

Now, let's discuss how you can practically support students in gaining this insight into algorithms and the broader structures of mathematics. To effectively foster structural insight and regularity in your students, you must guide them to recognize that algorithms are more than just sequences of steps to solve problems—they are profound tools that illuminate the underlying principles of mathematics. This approach helps students appreciate the elegance and utility of mathematical algorithms as conceptual frameworks that extend beyond routine calculations to model real-world phenomena and abstract ideas. The following sections provide you with detailed examples and strategies across different grade levels to ensure that this competency is directly applicable to classroom scenarios.

Introduce Algorithms as Conceptual Tools

Introducing algorithms as conceptual tools is a foundational approach in mathematics education that encourages students to understand and appreciate the underlying logic and structure of mathematical operations. By presenting algorithms this way, you help students see them not just as methods to achieve an answer but as tools that elucidate the deeper mechanisms of mathematics. This perspective is vital for cultivating a robust understanding across all grade levels. The following examples, beginning with elementary school, describe ways to accomplish this.

Structural Insight and Regularity

When teaching elementary students the concept of multiplication, introduce the algorithm alongside the area model to illustrate how multiplication can represent physical space and quantities. For example, if students are multiplying 5 by 3, use a grid or manipulatives to build a rectangle with one side measuring 5 units and another 3 units. As students fill in the grid, they count the total number of units (squares), which helps them visualize the product as 15. This method demonstrates the algorithm's role in organizing and visualizing mathematical concepts, making the abstract more tangible.

In middle school, teachers might try the following.

Deepen middle school students' understanding of algorithms by connecting them with the distributive property of multiplication over addition. Take the multiplication of a two-digit number by a single-digit number, such as 23 × 4. Break it down using the area model to show that 23 × 4 can be visualized as (20 + 3) × 4, which equates to (20 × 4) + (3 × 4). Use a rectangular array split into two sections to help students see how the distributive property works and how it simplifies multiplication. This approach reinforces the procedure and also explains why it works, enhancing students' ability to engage with algebraic expressions where similar distributive strategies are essential.

At the high school level, teachers could do the following.

Focus on algorithms within the context of algebra, particularly when solving quadratic equations. Introduce the quadratic formula as an algorithm, and use the discriminant to discuss its structure and implications. Illustrate how the formula $x = (-b \pm \sqrt{b^2 - 4ac}) \div 2a$ is derived from completing the square of a quadratic equation, and demonstrate its application to various quadratic equations. Discuss how the discriminant $b^2 - 4ac$ determines the nature of the roots (real or complex) and what this means graphically for the parabola represented by the equation. By connecting the algorithm to both its geometric interpretation and its derivation, students gain a comprehensive understanding of how algebraic algorithms function and the deeper mathematical principles they represent.

When you incorporate these examples into your teaching, you illustrate how algorithms serve as more than just tools for calculation; they are expressions of deeper mathematical concepts that students can use to navigate and understand the abstract and often complex landscape of mathematics. Research by Rittle-Johnson (2017) demonstrates that this methodological approach enhances students' computational fluency and their conceptual understanding. These findings are reinforced by Schneider and colleagues (2011), whose studies show that students who conceptually understand algorithms demonstrate greater mathematical flexibility and problem-solving capabilities. Furthermore, Powell and colleagues (2020) find through their synthesis of mathematics interventions that teaching algorithms with an emphasis on their underlying structures leads to more robust mathematical understanding and better preparation for advanced mathematical study.

Highlight Patterns and Structures

Highlighting patterns and structures in mathematical algorithms is a pivotal teaching strategy that deepens students' understanding of mathematical concepts and enhances their problem-solving skills. Regular classroom discussions that focus on the patterns and regularities within algorithms not only make abstract concepts more tangible but also illuminate the intrinsic beauty and logic of mathematics.

The following examples describe ways to approach this, beginning with an elementary classroom.

> In elementary grades, you can introduce the concept of patterns through the addition algorithm. For example, demonstrate addition with carryover using a set of problems that consistently result in carrying over, where the sum of the digits in any place is greater than 10. Show students how the pattern of carrying over to the next column simplifies calculations and ensures accuracy. Using manipulatives like base-ten blocks or drawing out the columns on paper could help students visualize the underlying structure of the addition process.

Middle school teachers could use the following approach.

For middle school students, explore the Euclidean algorithm, which is used to find the greatest common divisor of two numbers. Initiate the discussion by presenting a pair of numbers and working through the algorithm step by step. Highlight how each step of the algorithm systematically reduces the original pair of numbers until the greatest common divisor is revealed. Visualizing this repetitive reduction process through a flowchart or a series of steps on the board can help students recognize the regular pattern and understand how the algorithm simplifies complex problems through systematic reduction.

And high school teachers might do this.

In high school, leverage discussions about the patterns in the algorithm for solving linear equations, especially equations that involve multiple steps, such as combining like terms, moving variables to one side of the equation, and isolating the variable. Use a set of linear equations to show the regular structure of these steps. Discuss how this systematic approach helps students efficiently solve the equations and lays the groundwork for solving more complex algebraic equations. This can be enhanced with a SMART Board or software like algebra tiles where students can manipulate the equations, visually track the changes through each step, and see a consistent pattern emerge as they approach a solution.

By integrating these examples into your teaching, you can help students mechanically perform mathematical procedures as well as understand and appreciate the underlying patterns that make these algorithms effective and elegant. Research by Schneider and Stern (2010) demonstrates that this integrated approach significantly enhances both procedural fluency and conceptual understanding. Studies by Rittle-Johnson (2017) show that when students understand underlying patterns, they develop more flexible mathematical thinking and stronger problem-solving capabilities. Furthermore, Powell and colleagues (2020) find through their synthesis of mathematics interventions that teaching patterns alongside procedures not only reinforces computational skills but also fosters a deeper appreciation of mathematical structures, leading to more engaged and successful mathematics learners.

Encourage Generalization

Encouraging generalization in mathematics is a critical step in helping students transition from solving isolated problems to understanding broader mathematical principles. This process teaches them to identify common patterns and structures across different problems and to formulate general methods or rules that apply to an entire class of problems. It's a vital skill for developing a deep conceptual understanding of mathematics and for building the ability to think abstractly. Consider the following examples of this strategy in action, beginning with elementary school.

> In the elementary classroom, you can introduce generalization by using simple number patterns. For example, after students practice adding even numbers (like 2 + 4, 4 + 6, and 6 + 8), guide them to observe that the sum of two even numbers is always even. Challenge them to prove this rule with various pairs of even numbers and then discuss why this pattern holds, relating it to the structure of even numbers themselves. This exercise not only helps them solve addition problems but also deepens their understanding of number properties.

A middle school teacher might try something like this.

> Middle school students can explore generalization through geometry, such as by examining the relationships among the angles of different types of triangles. After measuring and adding the angles of several specific triangles and finding that they always sum to 180 degrees, students can be guided to formulate and justify the general rule that the sum of the angles in any triangle is 180 degrees. Encourage them to apply this rule to solve problems involving missing angles in triangles, thereby showing how a general principle can simplify the process of solving individual problems.

Structural Insight and Regularity

And a high school teacher might use the strategy in this way.

 In high school, generalization becomes particularly powerful in algebra. After students solve a variety of specific quadratic equations, you can encourage them to derive the general form of the quadratic formula. Start by guiding them through the process of completing the square for several quadratic equations, and then help them recognize the pattern that emerges. From these instances, lead a discussion that abstracts these observations into the general formula for solving any quadratic equation. This simplifies the task of solving any specific equation as well as helps students understand the underlying structure of quadratic relationships.

By fostering a classroom environment that encourages generalization, you empower students not just to learn mathematics by rote but to understand and apply mathematical concepts across various contexts. Studies by Schneider and colleagues (2011) demonstrate that this approach promotes a more robust understanding of mathematics, where students learn to connect discrete problems to general principles. Research by Rittle-Johnson (2017) shows that students who develop the ability to generalize mathematical concepts exhibit enhanced problem-solving capabilities and greater success with advanced mathematical challenges. Furthermore, Powell and colleagues (2020) find through their synthesis of interventions that this methodological shift from specific problem instances to broader conceptual thinking leads to improved mathematical outcomes across diverse student populations. These findings are reinforced by Cook and colleagues (2020), whose research indicates that teaching for generalization significantly enhances students' ability to transfer mathematical knowledge to new situations, fostering deeper appreciation for and mastery of the subject.

Explore Algorithm Variations

Exploring different algorithms for the same mathematical operation is an excellent strategy for deepening students' understanding of mathematical concepts and developing their ability to flexibly solve problems. By comparing various methods for performing operations such as multiplication, students can gain insights into how different algorithms work and why they might choose one method over another in different situations. Teachers at various levels can approach this strategy in different ways. In elementary school, students may respond to the following.

> In elementary grades, you can introduce students to different methods of multiplication through hands-on activities. For instance, demonstrate traditional column multiplication, lattice multiplication, and the use of a number line. With lattice multiplication, students create a grid that breaks down the multiplication process into smaller, more manageable parts, which helps them visualize a computation step by step. On the other hand, using a number line to multiply involves making jumps equivalent to one of the factors, repeated as many times as the other factor. This method can help students understand multiplication as repeated addition, which is a foundational concept.

Middle school teachers could encourage the exploration of algorithm variations in this way.

> In middle school, you can challenge students to apply these multiplication algorithms to more complex numbers and to explore their efficiency and practicality. For example, have students compare the speed and ease of traditional multiplication versus lattice multiplication when multiplying large numbers or decimals. Encourage discussion about which method feels more intuitive and why, and in what contexts one might be preferred over the other. This not only helps students practice the algorithms but also encourages them to think critically about the tools they use in mathematics.

And high school teachers could try the following.

> High school students can explore these multiplication algorithms in the context of algebra by applying them to polynomial multiplication. Show how different algorithms can be adapted for use with polynomials, such as applying the

lattice method to multiply binomials or trinomials. Discuss how the choice of algorithm might affect the simplicity and clarity of the solution, and encourage students to consider how these methods relate to the distributive property and to the graphical representation of polynomial functions.

In each case, discussing the advantages and limitations of each method encourages students to not only learn the mechanics of the algorithms but also understand the conceptual reasons behind them. Schneider and colleagues (2011) demonstrate that students who understand multiple solution methods develop greater procedural flexibility and deeper conceptual knowledge. This understanding also fosters flexibility in thinking, as students learn that there are multiple ways to approach a problem, each with its own benefits and drawbacks. Rittle-Johnson and Schneider (2015) show that this flexibility in approach significantly enhances students' problem-solving capabilities and mathematical reasoning. This understanding is crucial because it prepares students for more advanced mathematical studies and problem-solving scenarios, where flexibility and a deep conceptual understanding are paramount. According to Powell and colleagues (2020), students who develop this type of flexible thinking show greater success in transferring their mathematical knowledge to new and more complex contexts.

Apply Algorithms to New Contexts

Integrating algorithms into new contexts is a vital strategy for demonstrating the versatility and utility of mathematical procedures. By applying familiar algorithms to new types of problems or in interdisciplinary settings, students can see firsthand how mathematics intersects with other fields and real-world applications. This practice reinforces the concept that algorithms are more than just classroom exercises; they are powerful tools that can solve a wide range of practical problems. See the following examples, beginning with elementary school.

In elementary school, you can introduce students to the concept of applying algorithms in new contexts by incorporating simple real-world applications. For instance, use basic addition or subtraction algorithms to solve problems related to time, such as calculating the duration of events or the start and end times of activities. You could link this to daily routines or timetables, helping students see the practical use of these algorithms in managing their own schedules.

The next example describes the strategy for a middle school classroom.

For middle school students, extend the use of algorithms into subjects like science and geography. For example, teach them to apply the area calculation algorithms to determine the land area for different layers in a geography project, or use probability algorithms to analyze data from science experiments, such as predicting the outcomes of genetic crosses in biology or the probability of certain reactions in chemistry. This approach helps students understand the relevance of mathematical tools in scientific inquiry and data analysis.

And here is how you might approach applying algorithms to new contexts in high school.

In high school, the application of algorithms can be further expanded to include more complex interdisciplinary challenges. Encourage students to use algorithms for optimization, such as the shortest path algorithm for route planning in geography or cost minimization algorithms for problem solving related to budgeting and resource allocation in economics. Another example could involve applying statistical algorithms to interpret data in psychology or environmental science, helping students draw meaningful conclusions from empirical data.

In each of these scenarios, students practice transferring their mathematical knowledge to solve problems in varied contexts, thereby enhancing their problem-solving skills and reinforcing the idea that mathematics is a versatile and indispensable tool in their academic and future professional lives. Cook and colleagues (2020) demonstrate that this type of contextual transfer significantly improves students' ability to apply mathematical concepts across different domains. Studies by Powell and colleagues (2020) show that this approach not only solidifies students' understanding of the algorithms themselves but also broadens their perspective on where and how these mathematical tools can be applied. Furthermore, Rittle-Johnson (2017) finds that students who regularly engage with mathematics in varied contexts develop more flexible problem-solving strategies and demonstrate greater success in applying mathematical concepts to novel situations, fostering a deeper appreciation for the role of mathematics in the broader world.

Facilitate Reflective Discussions on Mathematical Structures

Incorporating reflective discussions about the underlying structures of mathematics can profoundly enhance students' understanding of why certain algorithms consistently yield correct results. Such discussions help students mechanically perform mathematical operations as well as appreciate the foundational principles that make these operations reliable. The following examples describe how to put this into practice, beginning with elementary school.

> In the elementary classroom, you can initiate these discussions by asking students to reflect on simple addition or subtraction methods. For example, after students use the traditional algorithm to add two numbers, ask them, "Why do we add the numbers from right to left starting with the units place?" and "What happens when these numbers add up to more than 9?" These questions can lead to a discussion on the place-value system and the concept of carrying over, which are fundamental to understanding the decimal system and its operation.

In middle school, try this.

> When middle school students learn about the distributive property of multiplication over addition, you can engage them in a discussion by asking, "Why does multiplying each addend by a number and then adding the results give the same answer as multiplying the entire sum by that number?" Such questions encourage students to think critically about the properties of operations and their implications, reinforcing their understanding of algebraic structures.

And for high school, students may benefit from the following.

>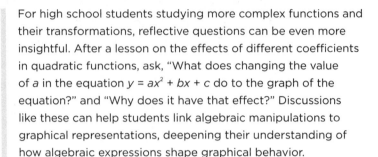
> For high school students studying more complex functions and their transformations, reflective questions can be even more insightful. After a lesson on the effects of different coefficients in quadratic functions, ask, "What does changing the value of *a* in the equation $y = ax^2 + bx + c$ do to the graph of the equation?" and "Why does it have that effect?" Discussions like these can help students link algebraic manipulations to graphical representations, deepening their understanding of how algebraic expressions shape graphical behavior.

These reflective discussions should be designed to not just review the steps of an algorithm but challenge students to think about the mathematical laws and properties that govern these steps. Rittle-Johnson (2017) demonstrates that such structured reflection significantly enhances students' conceptual understanding and mathematical reasoning abilities. By regularly integrating such discussions into your teaching, you encourage students to become more thoughtful and insightful mathematical thinkers. Studies by Heijltjes and colleagues (2014) show that this type of explicit reflection and discussion leads to improved critical thinking and deeper understanding of mathematical concepts. Furthermore, Powell and colleagues (2020) find that when students engage in regular mathematical discourse about underlying principles, they develop a coherent view of mathematics as a logical system, rather than as a collection of arbitrary rules, which enhances their reasoning and problem-solving skills.

By focusing on these strategies, you can effectively support your students in deeply understanding structural insight and regularity in mathematics and empower them to see beyond immediate problem solving to the beautiful patterns and structures that define the discipline.

Conclusion

In this chapter on structural insight and regularity within the CMC framework, we've delved deeply into how understanding the underlying structures and patterns of mathematics is not just an advanced skill but a fundamental aspect of learning mathematics at all levels. From elementary school introductions of algorithms as conceptual tools to high school discussions on the abstract structures that govern mathematical logic, each strategy and example provided aims to elevate students' understanding from merely solving problems to appreciating the mathematical principles that make these solutions possible.

The power of this competency lies in its ability to transform students' perspectives on mathematics. By moving beyond what's immediate and apparent, students begin to see mathematics as a coherent and interconnected system. This shift is crucial for fostering a deeper understanding of mathematics and for applying mathematical knowledge flexibly and innovatively across different contexts and problems. The emphases on generalization, exploration of algorithm variations, and application of algorithms to new scenarios all contribute to a dynamic learning environment where students are not just learners but young mathematicians in their own right.

Moreover, the reflective discussions on mathematical structures are instrumental in cultivating an appreciation for the elegance and efficiency of mathematical reasoning. These discussions encourage students to question and understand the why and how of the procedures they learn, which is essential for true mathematical fluency.

Our goal as educators is to guide students through this journey of discovery, helping them recognize and harness the patterns and regularities that make mathematics a powerful tool for interpretation and change in the world. Whether through hands-on manipulatives that lay the groundwork for understanding complex theories or through digital tools that connect abstract concepts to real-world applications, our teaching strategies must consistently aim to merge precision with insight.

In summary, structural insight and regularity are about both achieving correctness and fostering an analytical mindset that discerns and appreciates the deep structural insights within mathematical concepts. This chapter has outlined the practical methods to achieve these educational outcomes and has also highlighted the transformative impact of understanding and applying these structural insights in varied mathematical and real-world contexts. This comprehensive approach ensures that our students are proficient in mathematical procedures as well as capable of thinking critically and creatively about the mathematical challenges they will inevitably face beyond the classroom.

CHAPTER 8

Productive Disposition and Engagement

This chapter delves into the vital competency of productive disposition and engagement within the CMC framework. These elements center on cultivating a positive and enduring relationship with mathematics. Productive disposition encompasses the development of a mindset that views mathematics as logical, meaningful, and inherently valuable. It fosters the belief that diligent effort in learning mathematics yields substantial rewards and that each student is capable of achieving mathematical proficiency. Engagement, on the other hand, focuses on the active involvement of students in the learning process, encouraging them to persist through challenges and participate in their own learning. By conceptualizing productive disposition and engagement as a combined competency, the CMC framework provides educators with a structured approach to develop these elements simultaneously. Addressing them together allows for a more comprehensive cultivation of positive and active relationships with mathematics, which sets the stage for successful learning experiences across all mathematical competencies. This approach's strategies make mathematics meaningful and enjoyable for students, and thereby increase students' willingness to engage and persevere.

In the following pages, we'll explore how fostering a productive disposition and deep engagement enhances students' mathematical understanding and skills and also builds their confidence and resilience in facing mathematical challenges. Then, we'll examine strategies that effectively nurture these attributes to ensure students appreciate the utility and coherence of mathematics as well as see themselves as competent learners and doers of mathematics.

The Essence of Productive Disposition and Engagement

In the CMC framework, productive disposition and engagement are intertwined as a single competency because together, they form the emotional and attitudinal foundation that supports all other mathematics learning. This union is based on research suggesting that students' beliefs about their abilities significantly influence their engagement and success in mathematics.

According to the National Research Council (2001), a productive disposition toward mathematics is not just about having a positive attitude; it also encompasses believing that mathematics is comprehensible, useful, and worthwhile. This belief system supports engagement by motivating students to invest effort and actively participate in learning activities. Research continues to reinforce this understanding. Studies by Passolunghi and colleagues (2019) demonstrate how cognitive and emotional factors work together to influence mathematical engagement and achievement. This finding is further supported by Jessica M. Namkung, Peng Peng, and Xin Lin (2019), whose meta-analysis shows that students' beliefs about mathematics significantly impact their performance and persistence. Additionally, Sara A. Hart and Colleen M. Ganley (2019) find that when students see mathematics as accessible and relevant, they are more likely to engage deeply and persist through challenges, leading to improved mathematical outcomes.

Engagement, in this context, refers to students' participation in class activities as well as their intellectual involvement with mathematical concepts through explicit, systematic instruction. Research by VanDerHeyden and Codding (2020) demonstrates that effective engagement comes through structured learning experiences that build both skills and understanding. This type of systematic engagement is crucial for developing mathematical proficiency and the ability to accurately apply concepts across contexts.

The relationship between disposition and engagement must be understood within the context of evidence-based instruction. While positive attitudes can support learning, research by Li and Bates (2020) shows that the primary focus should be on developing mathematical competence through systematic skill building. This finding aligns with studies by Fuchs and colleagues (Fuchs, Newman-Gonchar, et al., 2021; Fuchs, Wang, et al., 2021) demonstrating that student success primarily comes from explicit instruction and structured practice; success in turn builds confidence and positive engagement with mathematics.

Moreover, research by Courtenay A. Barrett and Amanda M. VanDerHeyden (2020) emphasizes that effective mathematics instruction requires both systematic skill development and opportunities for active engagement with mathematical concepts. Teachers should create learning environments that provide clear instruction, structured practice, and appropriate support to build competence and confidence.

Productive Disposition Through Systematic Instruction

Studies by VanDerHeyden and Codding (2020) show that students' early experiences with mathematics are critical, but success depends more on receiving systematic, explicit instruction than on maintaining initial enthusiasm. Research by Powell and colleagues (2020) demonstrates that without structured, evidence-based instruction during these formative years, students may develop misconceptions and skill gaps that impede later learning. Furthermore, Morgan and colleagues (2015) find that effective early mathematics instruction focusing on systematic skill development helps prevent negative attitudes and builds a foundation for continued mathematical success.

The role of the mathematics teacher is pivotal in nurturing and sustaining a positive mathematical mindset among students. The way a teacher perceives and communicates the nature of mathematics—whether as a dynamic, accessible discipline or as a rigid, incomprehensible series of steps—profoundly influences their teaching practices. These practices, in turn, shape students' own beliefs about their mathematical abilities and the nature of mathematics itself.

Teachers and students collaboratively establish classroom norms that can significantly enhance or hinder a student's comfort and willingness to engage with mathematical concepts. When these norms promote an inclusive, supportive environment where students feel safe to explore ideas and learn from mistakes, students are more likely to view themselves as competent learners capable of understanding complex mathematical ideas.

This competency uniquely lends itself to teacher professional learning because it fundamentally involves the systematic analysis of both teaching and learning processes. Research by VanDerHeyden and Codding (2020) demonstrates that effective mathematics instruction requires teachers to continuously examine and refine their practices based on student responses and achievement data. Just as students must develop a productive disposition toward mathematics, believing in the coherence and comprehensibility of the subject and their own ability to master it, educators, too, must cultivate an evidence-based approach to instruction. This involves not just believing in students' capabilities but also systematically analyzing how instructional choices affect student learning outcomes.

Teachers should embrace the notion that their understanding of mathematics, insights into students' mathematical thinking, and teaching strategies are interconnected elements that can collectively enhance educational effectiveness. According to Powell and colleagues (2020), this systematic approach to examining teaching and learning empowers teachers to make data-driven decisions about instruction. Teachers with this analytical perspective see themselves as the architects of their own professional development, actively engaging in their educational growth by collecting and analyzing evidence of student learning and critically examining their teaching methods.

This reflective, evidence-based practice deepens teachers' understanding of how students' mathematical thinking evolves, as well as enriches their own mathematical knowledge through systematic analysis of classroom interactions. By adopting this approach, teachers can transform their classrooms into laboratories for improving instruction. Morgan and colleagues (2015) demonstrate that this ongoing analysis of student learning does not merely inform teachers about misconceptions or difficulties—it provides concrete evidence for refining instructional strategies and improving mathematical concept development. As a result, teachers become more confident and proficient in delivering effective mathematics instruction, paving the way for more structured and comprehensive understanding of mathematics. This self-sustaining cycle of systematic analysis and instructional refinement significantly contributes to more effective educational practice.

Teachers who embrace generative learning view themselves as life-long learners, capable of gaining valuable insights from a variety of sources, including curriculum materials and reflective practice. This perspective is critical, as it empowers teachers to continuously refine their pedagogical strategies and deepen their understanding of mathematics and student cognition. Research by Melissa Boston (2012) emphasizes that effective professional development empowers teachers to take an inquiry-oriented approach to improving their practice. She finds that when teachers analyze their own instructional methods and student interactions, they develop deeper content knowledge and more adaptive teaching strategies.

Additionally, a review by V. Darleen Opfer and David Pedder (2011) highlights that professional development is most impactful when it is embedded in teachers' daily work, allowing them to reflect on and refine their practice in an ongoing manner. They argue that this generative learning stance is crucial for helping teachers continually enhance their pedagogical skills and mathematical knowledge.

Furthermore, a study by Laura M. Desimone and Michael S. Garet (2015) reveals that professional development programs that encourage active learning, collective participation, and coherence with teachers' own goals and contexts are more likely to lead to changes in teacher practice and improved student outcomes. This aligns with the idea of empowering teachers to take charge of their own learning and development.

These studies continually reinforce the importance of the point made in earlier research—that effective professional development nurtures teachers as lifelong learners who can draw insights from their own practice and collaboration with peers, rather than simply deliver top-down solutions (Borko & Putnam, 1996; Loucks-Horsley, Stiles, Mundry, Love, & Hewson, 2010). Programs that merely offer ready-made solutions can inadvertently undermine this sense of agency, leading to passive reception of information rather than active engagement with the material. Such approaches fail to foster a productive disposition toward learning in mathematics education. Instead, effective professional development should challenge teachers to think critically and adaptively about their teaching strategies, and encourage them to experiment and learn from both successes and challenges.

In sum, the development of a generative learning stance in teachers is supported by professional development that values teacher autonomy, encourages reflective practice, and promotes deep engagement with both the material taught and the teaching methods used. This approach not only enhances teachers' mathematical knowledge and instructional skills but also reinforces their confidence in managing their own professional growth.

Engagement

Let's delve into the importance of maintaining high student engagement through strategic instructional scaffolding. Scaffolding, a teaching method that involves giving students the support they need while challenging them to go beyond their current skill level, plays a pivotal role in sustaining student interest and cognitive demand in mathematics.

For instance, consider how you, as a teacher, might scaffold a complex problem-solving task in a geometry class. Initially, you might guide students through a similar but simpler problem, providing hints and posing questions that lead students to consider different geometric properties and their relationships. As students become more comfortable with the concepts, you gradually reduce the support, allowing students to tackle more complex problems independently. This process not only keeps the task challenging and engaging but also encourages deep thinking and persistent effort among students.

Moreover, effective time management is crucial in keeping students engaged. Allocating just the right amount of time for tasks ensures that students remain focused without feeling rushed or overwhelmed. In a classroom scenario, this might mean you allow students ample time to discuss various solution strategies among themselves, giving them the opportunity to explore multiple approaches and deepen their understanding through peer interaction.

Another vital aspect of fostering engagement is your role in modeling high-level performance. By actively participating in discussions, demonstrating problem-solving strategies, and justifying mathematical procedures, you set a standard of excellence and reveal the value of persistence and precision in mathematical thinking. This both motivates students and shows them what is achievable with effort and dedication.

Last, pressing students for explanations and encouraging the development of meaning are essential for deep engagement. You should consistently challenge students to explain their reasoning and connect their solutions to broader mathematical concepts. This practice reinforces understanding as well as helps students develop a robust mathematical vocabulary and communication skills, crucial for success in academics and beyond.

In essence, engagement in mathematics is fostered not just through the selected tasks but through dynamic interactions among you, the students, and the tasks. A well-structured, supportive, yet challenging classroom environment is key to keeping students engaged and motivated in their mathematical pursuits.

Interplay Across Competencies

Teachers' professional growth in productive disposition and engagement uniquely positions this competency to influence all others within the CMC framework. Research by VanDerHeyden and Codding (2020) shows that teachers who systematically analyze their instructional practices develop stronger abilities across multiple domains.

When teachers deeply examine student learning processes, they enhance their own understanding of how conceptual knowledge and procedural knowledge develop (see chapter 2, page 25). According to Powell and colleagues (2020), this deeper teacher understanding leads to more effective explicit instruction that bridges concepts and procedures.

When it comes to problem solving and modeling (chapter 3, page 47), research by Doabler and colleagues (2015) demonstrates that teachers who actively analyze student problem-solving strategies develop more sophisticated approaches to modeling mathematical concepts. This analysis helps teachers create more effective scaffolding for complex mathematical tasks.

The competency of communication and representation (chapter 5, page 95) also finds support from productive disposition. According to Morgan and colleagues (2015), teachers who engage in systematic reflection about their practice develop the following.

- More precise mathematical language
- Better ability to represent concepts in multiple ways
- Stronger skills in addressing student misconceptions

Studies by Hughes and colleagues (2017) show that teachers who regularly reflect on instructional effectiveness make more strategic decisions about tool selection and implementation (see chapter 6, page 121). This reflection helps them do the following.

- Choose appropriate tools for specific learning objectives.
- Implement tools with greater precision.
- Adapt tool use based on student responses.

This multi-competency impact makes productive disposition and engagement particularly powerful for teacher development for the following reasons.

- It requires constant analysis of both teaching and learning.
- It directly connects to evidence-based instructional practices.
- It supports systematic improvement across all competencies.
- It aligns with research on effective mathematics instruction.

Strategies to Enhance Productive Disposition and Engagement

Developing a productive disposition and maintaining high levels of engagement in mathematics are critical for students' long-term success in the subject. Here are practical strategies you can use across different grade levels to cultivate this competency.

Create a Supportive Learning Environment

To effectively nurture students' mathematical abilities and attitudes, we need to implement strategies that are appropriate for their developmental stages. Here are some tailored approaches for different grade levels.

At the elementary level, try these approaches.

Promotion of questioning and curiosity: Develop classroom norms that actively encourage students to ask *why* and *how* questions without fear of being wrong. You can achieve this by framing mistakes as learning opportunities and consistently reinforcing that curiosity is valuable. For example, when a student attempts a difficult problem and finds an unconventional solution, highlight this effort in front of the class to show that creative thinking and persistence are as important as the correct answer.

Positive reinforcement: Use tools like reward systems or class recognition to celebrate not just correct answers but also the process of thinking and attempting problems. This

> reinforcement could include a Math Explorer of the Week award for a student who tries the most challenging problems or shows improvement in their mathematical thinking.

Middle school teachers can keep the following in mind.

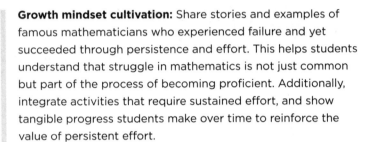

> **Growth mindset cultivation:** Share stories and examples of famous mathematicians who experienced failure and yet succeeded through persistence and effort. This helps students understand that struggle in mathematics is not just common but part of the process of becoming proficient. Additionally, integrate activities that require sustained effort, and show tangible progress students make over time to reinforce the value of persistent effort.
>
> **Group work dynamics:** Facilitate group projects or problem-solving sessions where students are grouped heterogeneously to learn from each other's strengths. Encourage rotating the roles within these groups, such as the explainer, challenger, recorder, and checker, to help all students participate actively and value different aspects of problem solving.

And in high school, the following approaches may benefit students.

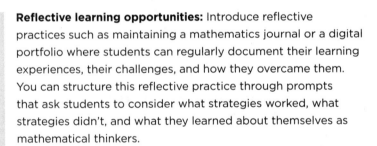

> **Reflective learning opportunities:** Introduce reflective practices such as maintaining a mathematics journal or a digital portfolio where students can regularly document their learning experiences, their challenges, and how they overcame them. You can structure this reflective practice through prompts that ask students to consider what strategies worked, what strategies didn't, and what they learned about themselves as mathematical thinkers.
>
> **Goal setting:** Encourage students to set short-term and long-term mathematical goals at the beginning of the school year. These goals could range from improving in a specific mathematical area, such as algebraic manipulations or geometric proofs, to achieving a particular score on a standardized test. Regular check-ins on these goals can help students remain engaged and see tangible progress in their mathematical journey.

By implementing these strategies, educators can create a learning environment that both supports and celebrates the ongoing development of each student's mathematical abilities and attitude.

Research has demonstrated that such supportive environments significantly enhance students' engagement and confidence in mathematics. For example, cultivating a growth mindset has been shown to improve academic achievement and resilience in students. A large-scale study by Yeager and colleagues (2019) finds that interventions promoting a growth mindset lead to higher grades and increased enrollment in advanced mathematics courses among high school students.

Promoting curiosity and positive reinforcement in the classroom can also increase students' motivation and interest in mathematics, which are critical factors for long-term engagement. Park and colleagues (2016) report that young students who are encouraged to explore and ask questions show greater mathematical achievement compared to those who do not experience such supportive instructional practices.

Furthermore, reflective learning practices, such as maintaining a mathematics journal, have been linked to improved critical thinking and problem-solving skills. Heijltjes and colleagues (2014) demonstrate that students who engage in explicit reflection combined with practice exhibit significant improvements in critical thinking abilities.

By integrating these research-backed strategies, educators both enhance students' engagement with mathematics and build a foundation of confidence and appreciation for the subject that can last a lifetime.

Enhance Student Engagement Through Active Learning Strategies

To cultivate a productive disposition and deep engagement in mathematics, integrating strategies that actively involve students in the learning process is crucial. These strategies enhance understanding and retention as well as make the learning experience more dynamic and inclusive. Here's how you can integrate some effective engagement strategies to transform the mathematical learning environment.

Charrette Protocol

Originally used in architecture, the Charrette protocol serves to refine student projects or problem solutions that have reached a standstill.

Implementation: When students or student groups find themselves unable to progress, they present their current work to the class or a selected group. The collective then engages in "working on the work," providing constructive feedback, suggesting alternative approaches, and brainstorming solutions to help overcome obstacles.

Benefit: This method cultivates a supportive classroom environment where students learn the value of collaboration and critical feedback. It encourages a culture of continuous improvement and collective problem solving, which is vital for maintaining engagement in challenging tasks.

Elementary students might use this strategy in the following way.

Implementation: When a group of students struggle to create a bar graph representing class pet preferences, they present their draft to the class. Classmates provide suggestions on labeling axes or choosing appropriate scales.

Benefit: Young students learn collaboration and receive immediate feedback to help them better understand data representation.

In middle school, students can use the strategy in the following way.

Implementation: Students working to design a simple budget for a school event share their calculations with peers when they encounter discrepancies. The class discusses possible errors in addition or allocation.

Benefit: This encourages analytical thinking and teamwork, which are vital for preteens developing more complex mathematical skills.

Productive Disposition and Engagement   173

And in high school, the strategy might appear this way.

Implementation: A group tackling a calculus problem that involves optimization presents their approach after hitting a roadblock. Peers offer insights on alternative methods or highlight calculation errors.

Benefit: This fosters a deep understanding of advanced concepts and promotes peer teaching.

Three-Act Math Tasks

Developed by Dan Meyer (2011), three-act math tasks engage students in real-world mathematical problems that are presented in a captivating three-act structure.

Implementation: The first act introduces a compelling scenario, the second act involves students in the problem-solving process, and the third act resolves the scenario and encourages reflection.

Benefit: These tasks contextualize mathematics in real-life situations, thereby enhancing students' analytical skills, fostering a deeper connection to the material, and making mathematics both accessible and engaging.

The following examples show how the acts might play out, beginning with elementary school.

Act 1: Show a video of a water tank being filled.

Act 2: Provide the rate at which water fills the tank and the tank's total volume.

Act 3: Reveal the time it takes to fill the tank, allowing students to compare that with their predictions.

Benefit: This makes abstract concepts like volume and rate tangible for young learners.

In middle school, the acts might look like this.

Act 1: Present a scenario where a stack of cups reaches a certain height.

Act 2: Give the measurement of one cup's height, and ask students how many cups are needed to reach the stack's specific height.

Act 3: Show the actual number of cups used.

Benefit: This enhances proportional reasoning and measurement skills.

And in high school, the strategy might play out in the following way.

Act 1: Display a video of a basketball shot and pause before the ball reaches the hoop.

Act 2: Provide data on the ball's initial velocity and angle.

Act 3: Show whether the shot was successful.

Benefit: This applies quadratic functions and projectile motion in a real-world context.

Jigsaw Method

In the jigsaw learning strategy, students in a home group all become experts on different segments of a topic.

Implementation: After mastering their segment, students discuss and enhance their understanding with other experts before teaching their home group.

Benefit: This method ensures active participation as students assume both learner and teacher roles, reinforcing their understanding and encouraging engagement from multiple perspectives.

In elementary school, the jigsaw method could look like this.

Implementation: Each student learns about a different basic shape (circle, square, or triangle) and teaches their group how to identify and draw it.

> **Benefit:** This builds foundational geometry skills and confidence in sharing knowledge.

In middle school, this method largely stays the same as the content gets more difficult.

> **Implementation:** Students specialize in different methods of solving linear equations (graphing, substitution, or elimination) and teach these methods to their peers.
>
> **Benefit:** This encourages mastery of multiple solution strategies and peer instruction.

And in high school, students can use this method to interact with even more complex mathematics.

> **Implementation:** Each student becomes an expert on a specific theorem in trigonometry and presents proofs and applications to their group.
>
> **Benefit:** This deepens understanding of complex concepts and enhances presentation skills.

Small-Group Learning

Utilize small groups to explore mathematical concepts through discussion, exploration, and collaborative learning.

> **Implementation:** These groups can work on various activities that foster mathematical thinking, such as constructing arguments, solving complex problems, and exploring mathematical models.
>
> **Benefit:** Small groups create safe spaces for students to express ideas, make mistakes, and learn from one another, which enhance their comfort and engagement with challenging material. This setup supports differentiated learning and helps students develop confidence in their mathematical abilities.

In elementary school classrooms, small groups give students opportunities to practice collaboration and get familiar with new perspectives on mathematics.

Implementation: Groups use manipulatives to solve basic addition and subtraction problems and discuss different ways to reach the answers.

Benefit: This encourages hands-on learning and foundational arithmetic skills.

In middle school, small groups can help students tackle nearly any concept.

Implementation: Students collaborate on a geometry project to calculate the area and perimeter of various shapes found around the school.

Benefit: This applies mathematical concepts to a real-world setting, thereby enhancing their relevance.

And in high school, as with other strategies, small groups help students digest ever more complex concepts.

Implementation: Groups tackle complex problems in statistics, such as analyzing datasets and interpreting standard deviations.

Benefit: This develops higher-order thinking and data-analysis skills.

Mathematical Tasks

Introduce tasks that challenge students to synthesize and apply their knowledge in new and complex ways.

Implementation: These tasks should involve significant thought, encouraging students to engage deeply with the content.

Benefit: High-level tasks promote critical thinking and problem-solving skills. They encourage students to understand the underlying mathematical principles and to apply these principles in novel situations.

Such tasks might play out for elementary students like this.

Implementation: Students create their own word problems using addition and subtraction, and then exchange with classmates to solve them.
Benefit: This enhances understanding of mathematical operations and language skills.

A middle school example might look like the following.

Implementation: Students design a simple business plan calculating costs, profits, and losses and integrate concepts of percentages and decimals.
Benefit: This applies mathematics to everyday financial literacy.

And in high school, the strategy might appear like this.

Implementation: Students use exponential functions to model population growth, analyze real-world data, and predict future trends.
Benefit: This connects advanced mathematical concepts to societal issues.

By incorporating these strategies, teachers can foster an environment where students are not just engaged but actively engaged in their learning. Research supports that active learning strategies significantly enhance students' engagement in and understanding of mathematics. For example, Nelson and McMaster's (2019) meta-analysis shows that early numeracy interventions involving active participation improve mathematical outcomes for preschool and early elementary students. These approaches help students develop a productive disposition toward mathematics, as students who engage in collaborative and hands-on activities tend to exhibit more positive attitudes toward the subject (Hwang & Riccomini, 2016). Moreover, active learning strategies have been shown to increase students' confidence and ability to handle mathematical challenges creatively. Heijltjes and colleagues (2014) find that students who participate in critical thinking activities combined with explicit instruction demonstrate significant improvements in problem-solving skills. By integrating these research-backed strategies, educators can create a dynamic and inclusive mathematical learning environment where students have the confidence and skills to creatively tackle complex mathematical problems.

Encourage Reflective and Critical Thinking

Fostering a reflective and critical mindset is essential for deepening students' mathematical understanding and enhancing their engagement. By encouraging students to reflect on their own thinking and to critically evaluate their problem-solving strategies, educators can significantly improve students' learning outcomes and their confidence in handling mathematical challenges. Consider the following approaches for different grade levels, beginning with elementary school.

> **Activity:** After completing a mathematics problem, engage students in a group discussion where each student shares their approach to solving the problem. Encourage them to use manipulatives or drawings to demonstrate their methods.
>
> **Benefit:** Young students learn to articulate their thinking processes, which helps them clarify their understanding and exposes them to diverse problem-solving methods from their peers. It also helps them build communication skills that are crucial for explaining mathematical concepts.

In middle school, teachers might try the following approach.

> **Activity:** Implement a "math congress" where students present their solutions to the class and receive feedback. Pose questions such as, "Why did you choose this method?" and "What might be the limitations of this approach?"
>
> **Benefit:** Middle school students are encouraged to think more deeply about the efficiency and effectiveness of their methods. This not only helps them understand the how and why behind their approaches but also promotes a culture of constructive criticism and self-improvement.

And in high school, the following method may benefit students.

Activity: Use case studies or real-world problems that require complex solutions. After they're solved, lead a discussion on the various strategies used and their outcomes. Encourage students to critique each approach, discussing potential improvements and alternative strategies.

Benefit: High school students develop advanced critical thinking skills by evaluating different mathematical approaches. This activity prepares them for higher education and professional environments where such skills are indispensable.

General strategies that teachers at all grade levels can keep in mind include the following.

Continuous reflection: Incorporate reflection into daily lessons, not just as a wrap-up activity but as an integral part of the learning process. This can be achieved through reflective journals, peer reviews, or digital portfolios where students record and reflect on their mathematical thinking over time.

Self-explanation: Motivate students to explain their reasoning aloud or in writing. This practice of self-explanation has been shown to significantly enhance learning because it compels students to clarify and justify their thought processes, which deepens their conceptual understanding.

By regularly integrating these reflective and critical thinking activities into the mathematics curriculum, teachers can help students develop a robust mathematical mindset. Fostering reflection and critical thinking significantly enhances students' mathematical understanding and problem-solving skills. For example, Rittle-Johnson and Schneider (2015) emphasize that self-explanation strategies compel students to clarify and justify their thought processes, leading to deeper conceptual understanding in mathematics.

Moreover, encouraging students to articulate their reasoning has been shown to improve their ability to transfer knowledge to new problems. A meta-analysis by Bethany Rittle-Johnson, Abbey M.

Loehr, and Kelley Durkin (2017) finds that prompting students to explain their solutions improves their problem-solving performance and flexibility in applying mathematical concepts. In addition, incorporating reflection into daily lessons helps develop students' metacognitive skills, which are linked to improved academic outcomes. According to Wolfgang Schneider and Cordula Artelt (2010), metacognition plays a crucial role in learning, and students who regularly reflect on their thinking processes tend to achieve higher levels of understanding and retention. By integrating these research-backed strategies, educators not only improve students' mathematical abilities but also foster lifelong engagement with mathematics, empowering students to become confident and capable mathematical thinkers.

Model and Demonstrate a Passion for Mathematics

An effective way to enhance students' engagement in and dispositions toward mathematics is for educators to demonstrate their own passion and appreciation for the subject. By showcasing the beauty, utility, and ubiquitous nature of mathematics, teachers can ignite a similar enthusiasm in their students. Consider the following example activities, beginning with elementary school.

Activity: Introduce mathematics through storytelling that incorporates mathematical concepts, such as counting adventures or shape-based puzzles. Highlight the role of mathematics in everyday contexts, like cooking (measuring ingredients) or playing sports (keeping score and statistics).

Benefit: Young students begin to see mathematics not as an abstract subject but as a living, breathing part of their daily lives. This approach helps them relate to the material more personally and see its value in everyday activities.

The following example focuses on middle school.

Activity: Use project-based learning to connect mathematics to real-world problems, such as budgeting for a class event and calculating the materials needed for a school project. Discuss how various professionals, from architects to video game designers, use mathematics.

Benefit: Middle school students are often motivated by practical applications. Seeing how mathematics applies to exciting careers and real-world challenges can spark a deeper interest and show them the practical benefits of acquiring strong mathematical skills.

And this one is designed for high school students.

Activity: Organize sessions where professionals from fields like engineering, data science, and economics talk about how they use mathematics in their jobs. Incorporate discussions on advanced mathematical concepts found in technology and science to illustrate cutting-edge applications.

Benefit: High school students considering their future careers can be greatly influenced by understanding the critical role that mathematics plays in high-demand fields. This exposure can motivate them to pursue higher-level mathematics courses and appreciate the subject's strategic importance.

Regardless of the grade level, teachers should consistently express their passion for mathematics through their teaching methods and interactions with students. Enthusiasm is contagious and can significantly alter students' attitudes toward the subject. Research by Passolunghi and colleagues (2019) demonstrates that teachers' enthusiasm significantly impacts students' mathematical engagement and achievement. This finding is reinforced by Hart and Ganley (2019), whose studies show that when teachers effectively communicate their passion for mathematics, students develop more positive attitudes toward the subject and show increased persistence on mathematical tasks.

Tailor lessons to include examples that align with students' interests. For instance, for students interested in the arts, discuss the role of geometry in visual art composition; for sports enthusiasts, explore statistical models in sports analytics. Studies by Hwang and Riccomini (2016) show that connecting mathematics to students' personal interests significantly increases engagement and retention. Regularly recognize and celebrate achievements in mathematics, not just correct answers but creative problem-solving approaches and improvements as well. According to Stevens and colleagues (2018), this type of recognition reinforces positive attitudes and encourages a culture of persistence and appreciation.

By embedding these strategies throughout the mathematics curriculum, educators can foster robust appreciation and lasting engagement among students. Research by Morgan and colleagues (2015) demonstrates that when teachers consistently model enthusiasm for mathematics while making meaningful connections to student interests, learners develop stronger mathematical identities and show improved academic outcomes. This approach enhances students' academic performance in mathematics as well as builds a lifelong positive disposition toward the subject.

Foster a Community of Mathematical Inquiry

Cultivating a supportive and inclusive classroom environment where students are encouraged to engage in mathematical discussions is essential for developing their understanding and appreciation of mathematics. Such an environment nurtures a community of inquiry that values curiosity, open dialogue, and collective learning. The following example activities help support mathematical inquiry, beginning with elementary school.

Activity: At this level, introduce math talk circles, where students sit in a circle and discuss a mathematics problem they worked on. Each student gets a chance to speak about their solution method or ask questions about parts they didn't understand.

Benefit: This strategy helps young learners feel valued and heard, encouraging them to express their mathematical thinking without fear of judgment. It promotes active listening skills and the ability to clearly articulate mathematical concepts.

In middle school, teachers can try the following.

Activity: Create a math wall where students can post questions, interesting mathematics facts, or challenges. This wall can serve as a focal point for weekly discussions, allowing students to lead conversations on selected topics.

Benefit: Middle school students begin to see the diversity of mathematical thought and to experience the benefit of collaborative learning. This ongoing interaction fosters a sense of community and encourages students to take ownership of their learning process.

And high school teachers might try this.

Activity: Implement regular peer-led teaching sessions where students prepare a mathematical concept or problem-solving technique and present it to their classmates. Provide a structured format that encourages questions and discussions to deepen understanding.

Benefit: High school students develop leadership and communication skills while reinforcing their mathematical knowledge. This peer teaching approach also helps demystify complex concepts and makes the learning process more relatable.

Consistently emphasize that questions and mistakes are natural and valuable parts of learning mathematics. Research by Schneider and colleagues (2011) demonstrates classrooms that normalize mathematical discourse and embrace mistakes as learning opportunities show significant improvements in student achievement. This finding aligns with work by Nicole M. Wessman-Enzinger and Natasha E. Gerstenschlager (2025) in *Celebrating Mathematical Mistakes*, which shows how creating a classroom culture that values mathematical discourse and views mistakes as opportunities for learning can transform students' mathematical understanding and confidence.

Studies by Powell and colleagues (2020) further support these benefits, showing that structured mathematical discussions significantly enhance both conceptual understanding and procedural fluency. Their research demonstrates that when students regularly engage in mathematical discourse, they realize the following benefits.

- Problem-solving abilities improve through exposure to diverse solution strategies.
- Mathematical vocabulary and communication skills develop more rapidly.
- Students show increased confidence in tackling challenging problems.
- Misconceptions are more effectively identified and addressed through peer discussion.

Morgan and colleagues (2015) find that establishing a community of mathematical inquiry leads to the following benefits.

- Deeper conceptual understanding through collaborative meaning making
- Enhanced mathematical reasoning through exposure to multiple perspectives
- Increased student engagement and participation
- Stronger mathematical identities among students

These findings reinforce the importance of creating classroom environments where mathematical discussion and collaborative learning are central to the educational experience. When students feel safe to take risks, ask questions, and learn from mistakes, they develop stronger mathematical skills and more positive attitudes toward mathematics as a discipline. Teachers should model this by sharing their own thought processes, including mistakes and corrections, during problem-solving sessions. Teach and reinforce norms for respectful dialogue. Ensure that every student understands how to give and receive constructive feedback, and how to appreciate different viewpoints and approaches in solving mathematical problems. Regularly dedicate time for students to reflect on what they've learned from discussions and how these discussions have influenced their understanding of mathematical concepts. Encourage students to give feedback on the discussion process to continually improve the dynamics of math talk circles and other activities.

Integrating these strategies helps students develop productive dispositions and engage so that they understand mathematical concepts and appreciate their value and relevance. By fostering a community of mathematical inquiry, educators can create a dynamic classroom atmosphere that encourages active participation and deep engagement with mathematical content. This holistic approach supports academic success, cognitive and social skills, and long-term relationships with mathematics to prepare students for thoughtful, analytical engagement with the modern world's challenges.

Conclusion

In this chapter, we've explored the profound roles of productive disposition and engagement within the CMC framework. This intertwined competency underscores the importance of fostering both a robust understanding of mathematical principles and persistent, positive engagement with mathematics throughout a student's educational journey.

Engagement in mathematics is cultivated through thoughtful instructional strategies that maintain high cognitive demand and provide supportive scaffolding. By implementing methods such as the Charrette protocol, three-act math tasks, and small-group activities, educators can create dynamic learning environments that encourage deep thinking and meaningful collaboration among students. These approaches ensure that mathematical tasks remain engaging and challenging, which is crucial for sustaining students' interest and involvement in their learning process. Similarly, developing a productive disposition requires more than just a positive attitude toward mathematics; it necessitates an educational environment where students believe in their capabilities and understand the value of perseverance. This belief is significantly influenced by how mathematics is taught and perceived in the classroom. Teachers play a pivotal role in this aspect by modeling enthusiasm for mathematics and by establishing a classroom culture that values curiosity, encourages risk taking, and views mistakes as learning opportunities.

Together, the elements of this competency create a powerful synergy that enhances students' ability to think critically and work collaboratively, equipping them with the confidence to tackle complex problems both in academic settings and in real-world contexts. By emphasizing the strategic use of various tools and techniques, we not only help students develop deeper mathematical proficiency but also prepare them to face future challenges with a resilient and proactive disposition. Ultimately, the journey through mathematics education should be one of continual growth and discovery. As educators, we have a goal to guide students to engage with mathematics all their life and see mathematical challenges as opportunities for innovation and personal development. This chapter has laid out foundational strategies to nurture these qualities, aiming to transform the mathematical landscape in ways that empower students to learn and to thrive.

CHAPTER 9

The CMC Framework in Your Classroom

This chapter explores the implementation of the CMC framework within your classroom, acknowledging the intricate and dynamic nature of fostering mathematical proficiency. This chapter is designed to provide you with actionable strategies to effectively implement the CMC framework, focusing on five critical elements to cultivate students' mathematical understanding and skills: (1) curriculum, (2) planning, (3) instruction, (4) assessment, and (5) professional learning.

Effective instruction is a cornerstone of this process, requiring a nuanced approach that adapts to the interactions among teachers, students, and the mathematical content. Through detailed examples and guidance, this chapter will show how to engage students in meaningful learning experiences that both enhance their immediate understanding and build a foundation for long-term mathematical thinking. Unit and lesson planning is another focal point of this chapter. Beyond mere lesson organization, effective planning involves deep contemplation of the mathematical content and a thorough understanding of your students' cognitive development and learning needs. This strategic planning must align with the goals of the CMC framework to cohesively develop all seven competencies across your curriculum. The chapter also explores methods of assessment that support the CMC framework. Effective assessment practices are crucial for gauging student progress, informing instructional decisions, and enhancing student learning. I discuss how to design and implement assessments that not only evaluate student understanding but also encourage deeper engagement with mathematical concepts.

Finally, professional development is essential for successful implementation of the CMC framework. This includes fostering deep content knowledge, understanding pedagogical strategies that support mathematical thinking, and preparing to modify teaching approaches based on student feedback and educational research.

By integrating these five critical elements, this chapter aims to equip you with the necessary tools to create a robust mathematical learning environment and foster comprehensive mathematical proficiency. This environment will address your students' immediate educational needs as well as prepare them for future academic challenges and everyday problem solving.

Curriculum

Mapping the seven competencies of the CMC framework onto the existing scope and sequence in mathematics education involves strategic alignment that enhances the curriculum.

Scope-and-Sequence Implementation

Each competency can be woven into the diverse content areas listed in a scope-and-sequence document with common units to bolster the depth and applicability of mathematics learning. The following example covers grades K–5.

1. Conceptual and Procedural Integration

Kindergarten: Introduce addition and subtraction concepts within 10 (units 5, 6, and 7) using varied examples and manipulatives that demonstrate the merging of conceptual understanding with procedural fluency.

Grade 3: During the exploration of multiplication as repeated addition (units 3, 4, 5, and 11), emphasize conceptual models like arrays alongside traditional algorithms to deepen understanding.

2. Problem Solving and Modeling

Grade 2: In units dealing with word problems that involve addition and subtraction (units 3, 6, and 10), integrate problem-solving strategies and modeling techniques to show real-world application of these operations.

Grade 5: Apply problem solving to fractions and decimals (units 9, 10, and 11), encouraging students to use models and diagrams to visualize and solve more complex problems.

3. Logical Reasoning and Proof

Grade 4: In units where properties of operations are taught (units 3, 5, 9, and 10), have students create arguments or proofs that demonstrate why certain mathematical properties hold true using logical reasoning.

4. Communication and Representation

Grade 1: While exploring basic number operations (units 5, 6, and 7), use various communication methods and representations such as drawings and physical models to clarify mathematical ideas.

Grade 5: Enhance understanding of operations with fractions (units 9, 10, and 11) by encouraging students to represent problems in multiple ways, including number lines and area models.

5. Strategic Use of Tools and Precision

Grade 3: Integrate the use of rulers and other measurement tools (units 6 and 7) to teach precision in measurement and to solve problems accurately.

Grade 5: When dealing with decimals and fractions (units 9, 10, and 11), focus on the precision of decimal placement and fraction equivalence using tools like fraction strips and decimal grids.

6. Structural Insight and Regularity

Grade 2: Highlight patterns in addition and subtraction (units 2, 3, and 4) to build a foundation for recognizing mathematical structures and regularities.

Grade 4: Discuss the structure of number systems in base-ten operations (units 2, 6, and 7) to deepen students' insight into the decimal system and its regularities.

7. Productive Disposition and Engagement

Kindergarten to grade 5: Throughout all units, continuously foster an environment that encourages curiosity, resilience, and a positive disposition toward mathematics. Celebrate efforts and strategies as much as correct answers to maintain high student engagement.

By systematically aligning these competencies with the existing scope and sequence, educators can ensure that the mathematics education they provide is comprehensive, interconnected, and deeply enriching for students across all elementary grades. This approach covers the breadth of mathematical topics as well as deepens the quality of learning experiences, which ensures that students are well equipped for future mathematical challenges. The following describes how the seven competencies work with a grades 6–12 scope and sequence with common units.

1. Conceptual and Procedural Integration

Grade 6: Focus on ratio concepts and proportional relationships (units 1, 2, and 3) to demonstrate the integration of conceptual understanding with procedural fluency through real-world examples and ratio tables.

Grade 9: Emphasize the link between algebraic expressions and their geometric representations in linear and quadratic functions (units 2 and 4) to solidify understanding through both symbolic manipulation and graphing.

2. Problem Solving and Modeling

Grade 7: Apply problem-solving strategies to statistics and probability (units 5 and 6), encouraging students to model

The CMC Framework in Your Classroom

situations and analyze data through simulations and graphical representations.

Grade 12: Tackle calculus problems (units 2, 3, and 4) that involve limits, derivatives, and integrals, using modeling to connect abstract concepts to physical phenomena like motion and area.

3. Logical Reasoning and Proof

Grade 8: Engage students in proving geometric properties (units 6, 7, and 8), using deductive reasoning to establish relationships between different geometric figures.

Grade 10: Deepen understanding of congruence and similarity in geometry (units 1, 3, and 4) through formal proofs and logical arguments.

4. Communication and Representation

Grade 6: Enhance discussions on numerical operations and fractions (units 3, 4, and 5) by using multiple forms of representation, such as graphs, tables, and verbal explanations.

Grade 11: Discuss advanced algebraic and trigonometric functions (units 2, 4, and 5) through various forms of communication, including symbolic, graphical, and numerical representations.

5. Strategic Use of Tools and Precision

Grade 7: Incorporate the use of digital tools like graphing calculators and geometry software (units 1, 2, and 8) to teach precision in plotting points and drawing accurate graphs.

Grade 12: Focus on calculus and statistics (units 2, 3, and 5), emphasizing the strategic use of tools like computer algebra systems and statistical software to enhance precision in solving complex problems.

6. Structural Insight and Regularity

Grade 8: Explore patterns in number systems and algebraic structures (units 1, 5, and 7), helping students recognize underlying mathematical frameworks.

Grade 11: Delve into the periodicity of trigonometric functions and the structure of polynomial roots (units 3 and 4), linking these concepts to their algebraic and graphical properties.

7. Productive Disposition and Engagement

Grades 6–12: Throughout all units, maintain a classroom environment that encourages a positive outlook toward mathematics. Implement strategies that promote engagement and belief in the usefulness and sensibility of mathematics, such as presenting mathematics in context with real-world applications and giving students opportunities to confidently express mathematical ideas.

As with the elementary example, careful alignment of competencies and the scope and sequence means middle and high school mathematics educators can provide a comprehensive, interconnected, and deeply enriching educational experience. This approach both covers the breadth of mathematical topics and enhances the quality of learning experiences, effectively preparing students for future academic and career challenges.

Ideally, the seven competencies of the CMC framework should be seamlessly integrated and evident in every lesson to provide a robust and holistic mathematics education. However, the preceding mapping serves as an example of how these competencies can be emphasized at the unit level, demonstrating their integration into the broader scope and sequence of the curriculum.

Although it's advantageous for each lesson to touch on multiple competencies, it's also strategic to highlight specific competencies within certain units to ensure deep coverage and mastery. This approach allows for a focused exploration of each competency within the context of relevant mathematical content, which ensures that students have comprehensive understanding of specific skills and knowledge and can apply these skills across different mathematical domains. For example, while a lesson on fractions might primarily focus on the competencies of problem solving and modeling and communication and representation, it would also ideally incorporate elements of structural insight and regularity to help students see the underlying patterns in fraction operations. Similarly, a unit on geometry could emphasize logical reasoning and proof and strategic use of tools and precision, while still fostering productive disposition and engagement through interactive and challenging tasks.

The goal is to make all seven competencies integral parts of the learning experience, woven into the fabric of daily mathematical discussions and activities. By doing so, teachers ensure that students are learning mathematics in an engaging and meaningful way as well as developing a versatile and durable mathematical proficiency that will serve them well beyond their school years. This integrated approach also ensures that students recognize the interconnectedness of different mathematical ideas and competencies, which enhances their overall mathematical fluency and problem-solving capabilities.

Curriculum Alignment

Adopting the CMC framework doesn't require overhauling your existing resources or textbooks. Instead, it involves strategically using these resources to emphasize and develop the desired competencies. Here's a pragmatic guide to how teachers, individually or in teams, can align textbook exercises with the CMC framework to enhance their effectiveness.

1. Review and select suitable problems.

    a. **Identify key concepts:** Start by identifying the key concepts covered in your textbook that align with each of the seven comprehensive mathematical competencies. For example, locate sections where problem solving, logical reasoning, and use of mathematical tools are emphasized.

    b. **Evaluate existing problems:** Assess the problems in these sections to determine whether they challenge students to think critically, use tools strategically, or apply concepts in novel ways. Look for problems that require more than rote calculation and that encourage reasoning and justification.

c. **Share findings:** In department meetings or collaborative planning sessions, share the problems you've identified with your peers. Discuss how these problems align with the comprehensive mathematical competencies.

d. **Create a repository:** Develop a shared digital document or database where teachers can contribute textbook problems that align with specific competencies. This resource can grow over time and serve as a valuable tool for all teachers in the department.

2. Modify and elevate questions.

a. **Adapt questions:** Modify textbook questions to better reflect the depth required by the comprehensive mathematical competencies. For example, add a requirement for students to explain their reasoning or to use a specific tool or representation method.

b. **Design follow-up questions:** Create follow-up questions that push students to further explore concepts or apply their knowledge in new contexts, enhancing engagement and understanding.

c. **Organize workshop sessions:** In regular workshops, have teachers present how they have adapted textbook questions. These sessions can serve as brainstorming opportunities to collectively elevate questions to meet CMC standards.

d. **Solicit peer review:** Use team meetings to review and critique adapted problems, ensuring they are challenging and well aligned with intended competencies.

The CMC Framework in Your Classroom 195

3. Plan for implementation.

    a. **Sequence:** Determine where and how the adapted or selected problems will fit into your lesson plans. Ensure there is a logical progression that builds on students' existing knowledge and skills.

    b. **Document:** Keep a personal teaching journal to note observations on how students respond to these problems, what works well, and what needs adjustment.

    c. **Share lesson plans:** Develop and share lesson plans that incorporate the adapted problems. Team members can try these plans and provide feedback based on their experiences.

    d. **Hold reflective meetings:** Use regular meetings as opportunities to discuss the effectiveness of using these problems in the classroom. Discuss student responses, engagement levels, and areas for improvement.

4. Prioritize continuous improvement.

    a. **Gather student feedback:** Regularly solicit feedback from students about the clarity and challenge of the problems. Use this feedback to further refine problem selection and adaptation.

    b. **Engage in professional development:** Use professional development sessions focused on effective problem selection and adaptation strategies to widen learning within the CMC framework.

    c. **Conduct action research:** Utilize small-scale research projects within your team to test the effectiveness of different strategies for aligning textbook problems with the comprehensive mathematical competencies.

By taking these steps, teachers can effectively integrate the CMC framework into their existing curriculum using the textbooks they already have. This approach both maximizes resources and fosters a collaborative, reflective, and dynamic teaching environment. Such a collective effort helps maintain a high standard of mathematics teaching and learning, thereby ensuring that all students develop strong mathematical competencies.

Planning

Effective instruction is pivotal in cultivating mathematical proficiency. This does not prescribe a single method; rather, it emphasizes the need for a flexible approach that considers the interplay among teachers, students, and the mathematical content. High-quality instruction hinges on teachers' deep understanding of mathematical content, their awareness of how students learn, and their ability to engage students in meaningful tasks. To achieve this, you must continuously refine your teaching strategies based on keen observation of students' responses and ongoing evaluation of their understanding and engagement.

The planning phase of instruction is often underestimated in its complexity. Effective planning requires thoughtful consideration of the mathematical content and a deep understanding of your students' current knowledge and learning trajectories. Here, the goal is to develop a comprehensive plan that not only addresses the immediate instructional goals but also builds toward a broader understanding of key mathematical concepts.

Incorporating the seven competencies of the CMC framework into your classroom planning involves a holistic approach that spans content, methodology, and assessment. Here's how you can effectively integrate these competencies into your lesson planning to enhance the depth and applicability of mathematics learning.

- **Content and goals:** Align with big ideas and instructional goals.
  - *Conceptual and procedural integration*—When planning lessons, especially on complex topics like fractions

The CMC Framework in Your Classroom

and algebra, ensure that the materials and tasks not only teach the procedures but also help students understand the underlying concepts. For example, when introducing algebraic expressions, use materials that relate algebra to arithmetic students already understand to show the continuity of concepts.

- *Problem solving and modeling*—Select tasks that require students to apply mathematical concepts to real-world problems. This could be as simple as using geometric shapes to solve space allocation issues in project-based learning scenarios, which helps illustrate the utility of geometry in practical contexts.

- *Logical reasoning and proof*—Include opportunities for students to engage in activities where they must formulate and justify their reasoning, such as proving geometric theorems or validating algebraic manipulations through logical arguments.

- *Communication and representation*—Choose tasks that encourage students to express mathematical ideas in multiple forms (verbally, numerically, graphically, and symbolically). For example, when teaching data handling, have students present the same dataset through different types of graphs and discuss the advantages of each.

- *Strategic use of tools and precision*—Incorporate the use of appropriate mathematical tools, such as statistical analysis software or dynamic geometry tools, to enhance precision in calculations and representations.

- *Structural insight and regularity*—Plan lessons that highlight mathematical structures or patterns, such as the periodicity in trigonometric functions or the pattern in the number of diagonals of polygons. This helps students appreciate the beauty and order within mathematics.

- *Productive disposition and engagement*—Design activities that build confidence and foster an interest in mathematics, such as collaborative projects or competitions that involve creative use of mathematical concepts.
- **Student-centered approach:** Tailor your approach to individual needs and interests.
  - Adopt adaptive teaching strategies that cater to the diverse learning styles and paces of your students. Start each unit with diagnostic tasks to gauge prior knowledge, and continuously use formative assessments to monitor progress.
  - Differentiate instruction to provide various entry points into a topic that cater to students' unique backgrounds and abilities. This could mean giving additional scaffolding for those who need more support or offering enrichment tasks for advanced learners.
- **Continuity and integration:** Create coherent learning journeys.
  - Ensure that each lesson is not an isolated event but part of a continuum that builds on previous knowledge and leads into subsequent topics. This is particularly important in mathematics, where concepts are highly interconnected.
  - Plan for lessons to reinforce earlier concepts, using them in new and more complex applications. For example, earlier lessons on linear equations can be extended to systems of equations in higher grades, showing progression in the use of algebraic methods.
  - Make explicit connections between topics that might initially seem disparate to help students see mathematics as a unified body of knowledge. For instance, link the probability calculations in statistics to algebraic formulas for combinations and permutations.

By thoughtfully incorporating these elements into your planning, you can ensure that your instruction not only covers the required curriculum but also enriches students' mathematical experiences and builds their proficiency across all seven competencies of the CMC framework. This approach enhances academic performance as well as prepares students to apply mathematical thinking in varied real-world contexts.

Regularly demonstrate how to approach problems, think critically, and make connections between different mathematical ideas. This modeling helps students develop their own problem-solving strategies and understand the value of persistence and precision in mathematical thinking. By focusing on these aspects, you are not just teaching mathematics; you are guiding your students toward a deeper, more integrated understanding of the subject that goes beyond mere procedural knowledge. This approach supports the immediate learning objectives, and it prepares students for lifelong engagement with mathematics, fostering both their cognitive and dispositional growth.

Instruction

Before delving into the practical application of the CMC framework within your classroom, it's vital to thoughtfully structure each lesson to maximize student learning and engagement. Interaction within the classroom is another critical consideration.

Lesson Design

The lesson design template provided in figure 9.1 (page 200) is crafted to seamlessly integrate the CMC framework into your daily teaching practices to ensure that every lesson is robust and effective.

The following sections will explain each component of the lesson design template to help you understand how to effectively utilize the template in your planning and execution. Your district may already have requirements for lesson and unit plans, but adopting a new template focused on the CMC framework can rejuvenate your instructional approach and enhance the educational experience for both you and your students.

MATHEMATICS TEACHING REIMAGINED

Preparation for the Lesson	
Unit or Lesson	Integer Exponents Date: 10/22
Essential Learning Standard	"Know and apply the properties of integer exponents to generate equivalent numerical expressions" (8.EE.A.1).
Learning Target	Students will be able to correctly apply the laws of exponents to simplify expressions.
Academic Language	*Exponent, base, power, product of powers, quotient of powers, power of a power*
Beginning-of-Class Routines	
Warm-Up	Time: 10 minutes Activate prior knowledge about multiplication and division of numbers and how these operations relate to exponents. Engage students in a quick review task where they multiply and divide small numbers to refresh these concepts.

During-Class Routines
(One or more instructional activities)

What will the teacher be doing?

Launch: Introduce the specific laws of exponents (product of powers, quotient of powers, power of a power) with examples on the board.

Scaffold for understanding: Use visual aids and interactive demonstrations to explain exponent rules.

Extension for advanced learners: Challenge students with negative exponents and fractional bases through advanced problem sets.

Student engagement strategy: Implement think-pair-share for each new exponent rule introduced.

Logical reasoning and proof competency of the CMC framework: Encourage students to articulate and defend their understanding of how exponent rules work and to analyze and respond to the explanations provided by their peers.

What will the students be doing?

Engagement: Students participate in discussions and hands-on activities, using interactive tools like graphing calculators or software to visualize exponent rules.

Discourse requirement: Small-group discussions facilitate deeper understanding and explanation of processes.

Mathematical thinking development: Develop conceptual and procedural integration by connecting exponent rules to previous knowledge of multiplication and division.	
Task 1	Task: Applying product of powers Time: 15 minutes CMC focus: Problem solving and modeling Activity details: Students solve real-world problems (for example, calculating exponential growth) with the product of powers rule, using technology to model these relationships graphically.
Task 2	Task: Exploring quotient of powers Time: 15 minutes CMC focus: Conceptual and procedural integration Activity details: Students work through guided problems that require simplifying expressions using the quotient of powers rule, and then correct common misapplications of the rule, enhancing understanding of both concept and procedure.
Task 3	Task: Exploring power of a power Time: 20 minutes CMC focus: Communication and representation Activity details: Students create visual representations of the power of a power rule using digital tools and explain their models in small groups before presenting to the class, which encourages peer feedback and deeper communication.
Closure Routines	
Structured Closure Routine	**Targeted Exit Task** Time: 10 minutes Task focus: Students complete a partially worked example that combines multiple exponent rules (for example, product and quotient of powers). Students identify errors in a given solution, correct them using proper notation, and prove their answer by showing each step. This structured format reveals specific misconceptions about exponent rules and provides clear evidence of procedural and conceptual understanding to inform tomorrow's instruction.

Figure 9.1: Lesson design template.

continued on next page →

Common Independent Practice (Blocked and Interleaved)	Provide problems that incorporate all three exponent rules, ranging from simple to complex, to reinforce learning and encourage application of today's lesson.
Evidence of Learning (Assessments)	Give a quick quiz at the end of the lesson to assess understanding of exponent rules and their applications.
Teacher End-of-Lesson Reflection	Problem solving and modeling: Today's lesson centered on multiplying fractions using visual models such as area models and number lines. The effectiveness of the lesson was evident as students actively engaged in constructing their own area models to represent fraction multiplication. This hands-on approach allowed students to see the intersections of shaded areas as a practical demonstration of how fraction products are derived. Students were particularly effective in using models to solve word problems that required multiplication of fractions, indicating a strong grasp of the conceptual underpinning of the operation. Challenges: A common challenge observed was the difficulty some students faced in transitioning from visual models to more abstract representations, such as writing the multiplication equation that corresponded to the model. Several students also had misconceptions about the multiplication of fractions larger than 1, where the product ends up being smaller than the factors. To address these challenges in future lessons, I plan to integrate more bridging activities that explicitly connect visual models to symbolic representations. This will include guided practice where, together, we draw the model, write the equation, and discuss the relationship between the two. Additionally, I will design a minilesson specifically targeting the concept of multiplying fractions greater than 1, using real-world contexts to solidify understanding.

Source for standard: NGA & CCSSO, 2010.

*Visit **go.SolutionTree.com/mathematics** for a free reproducible version of this figure.*

The CMC Framework in Your Classroom 203

Preparation for the Lesson

Before stepping into the classroom, you must have a clear blueprint of what the lesson entails. This starts with specifying the unit or lesson focus and the date, which helps in chronologically organizing the curriculum. The essential learning standard involved should align with state, provincial, or national standards and provide a clear framework of the expected learning outcomes. The learning target clarifies the specific objectives for the lesson, detailing what students should know and be able to do by the end of the session. This is complemented by academic language, where you identify and plan to introduce the key vocabulary and concepts that are critical to students' successful engagement with the lesson's content.

Beginning-of-Class Routines

The start of the class sets the tone for learning. A warm-up activity is crucial because it activates prior knowledge and prepares students for the new concepts they will encounter. This activity should directly relate to the lesson's content, serving as a bridge between previous learning and the day's objectives.

During-Class Routines

This section of the template is divided into two main parts: (1) what the teacher will be doing and (2) what the students will be doing. As the educator, your actions should include a launch, where you introduce tasks by connecting them to relevant comprehensive mathematical competencies such as problem solving and modeling. Scaffolding for understanding includes providing targeted questions and support for students who may struggle while also offering extension for advanced learners to keep all students challenged. The student engagement strategy should ensure that all students are actively participating in the learning process.

On the students' side, engagement activities should involve them in active learning through methods like collaborative problem solving, which enhances their skills in communication and representation. The discourse requirement should specify the nature of discussions and promote a rich exchange of ideas that supports productive disposition and engagement. The part on mathematical thinking development should outline how the activities will enhance specific comprehensive mathematical competencies.

Each task should be time bound and aligned with specific comprehensive mathematical competencies to ensure that activities are both productive and purposeful. Detailed instructions should guide the students through the learning process, helping them efficiently meet the set objectives.

Closure Routines

End each lesson with structured exit tasks that require students to demonstrate specific mathematical understanding. Rather than general summaries, use partially worked examples with strategic gaps, targeted problem-solving tasks, or error-analysis activities that provide concrete evidence of learning. Students should engage with these tasks individually, showing their mathematical thinking through precise vocabulary and multiple representations. Use the resulting data to identify specific misconceptions and inform the next day's instruction, including student grouping and targeted interventions. This structured approach reduces cognitive load while strengthening learning through retrieval practice and immediate, specific feedback.

Focus on demonstrable understanding rather than perceived confidence, avoiding vague prompts or self-assessments. By implementing these research-based closure routines systematically, you create an environment where mathematical proficiency develops through careful attention to both procedural fluency and conceptual understanding, supported by concrete evidence of student learning.

Classroom Interaction

In the classroom, the interaction among the teacher, the students, and the mathematical tasks should be dynamic and responsive. This interaction is crucial for effective learning, as it helps students engage with the content as well as develop the cognitive and metacognitive skills necessary for deep mathematical thinking. Be prepared to adapt your teaching strategies based on student responses during lessons. This might mean providing additional challenges for students who are ready or offering targeted support where difficulties arise.

Classroom interaction plays a pivotal role in cultivating a learning environment conducive to deep exploration of mathematical concepts. To effectively foster such an environment, it is essential to create a classroom atmosphere where students feel safe to engage in exploration, ask questions, and even make mistakes without fear of judgment. You can achieve this by establishing clear norms that value curiosity, respect diverse thinking, and see errors as opportunities for learning.

Encouraging open discussions is a key strategy in this context. Teachers should facilitate conversations that prompt students to articulate their thought processes, justify their reasoning, and actively listen to and learn from their peers. For example, after presenting a mathematical problem, a teacher might ask students to share their different approaches to solving it. During this discussion, students can explain their reasoning, ask clarifying questions, and constructively critique each other's methods. This deepens their understanding and also helps them see the value in diverse problem-solving strategies.

Moreover, incorporating activities that require students to work in small groups or pairs can further enhance this interactive learning process. In these settings, students can tackle problems together, freely discuss their ideas, and provide peer feedback. You have a crucial role here in guiding these interactions to ensure they remain productive and focused on the mathematical content.

Such an approach not only improves students' mathematical skills but also boosts their confidence in handling complex ideas. It transforms the classroom into a dynamic space where mathematics is seen as a collaborative and engaging discipline and students are encouraged to take risks and approach problems with a resilient and investigative mindset. By continually supporting and refining these interaction strategies, teachers can help students build a robust foundation in mathematical thinking and communication.

Assessment

Formative assessments are essential tools for educators to measure and enhance students' grasp of mathematical concepts and their proficiency in applying these concepts through the CMC framework. The purpose of formative assessments is not merely to evaluate what students know but, more importantly, to illuminate how they think, reason, and solve problems. This aligns directly with the goals of the CMC framework, which emphasizes a holistic approach to learning mathematics that integrates conceptual understanding, procedural skills, and the strategic application of tools and reasoning.

Formative assessments provide real-time feedback to both teachers and students, offering insights that are crucial for adjusting teaching strategies and supporting students in their learning journeys. These assessments are designed to be integrative, pulling in elements from each of the seven competencies outlined in the CMC framework—ranging from problem solving and modeling to logical reasoning and the strategic use of tools. By embedding these competencies into the assessment process, teachers can foster a more dynamic and responsive learning environment.

Assessments should encourage students to articulate their reasoning, model mathematical concepts, and apply these concepts in various contexts to significantly enhance their understanding and retention of the material. Developing an assessment that aligns with a proficiency scale provides a structured approach to evaluating student progress and understanding. This approach ensures that assessments are means of measuring progress as well as powerful pedagogical tools to advance students' mathematical thinking and engagement. The following sections share a few examples that incorporate both formative assessment and a corresponding proficiency scale. These clear examples will guide you through the process of crafting these assessments and proficiency scales.

Formative Assessment Example: Understanding Proportions

This formative assessment example integrates multiple competencies from the CMC framework, particularly focusing on problem solving and modeling, communication and representation, and conceptual and procedural integration. The real-world context challenges students to apply their understanding of proportional relationships while demonstrating their ability to represent mathematical thinking in multiple ways. By requiring students to calculate quantities, create visual models, and explain real-world applications, this assessment evaluates students' procedural fluency alongside their conceptual understanding of proportions. The task specifically supports these competencies in the following ways.

- Problem solving and modeling through the application of proportional reasoning in a practical context
- Communication and representation through the creation and explanation of proportional models
- Conceptual and procedural integration through the connection of numerical calculations with visual representations
- Strategic use of tools and precision through accurate calculations and appropriate use of digital tools
- Productive disposition and engagement through relevant real-world connections

Assessment task: Students receive a real-world scenario where they need to apply their understanding of proportions to solve problems. The task challenges them to find solutions and also to model their thinking using appropriate mathematical representations.

Scenario: The school cafeteria plans to prepare a special lunch for 150 students. The recipe provided is for 50 servings. Students need to calculate the quantities of the ingredients needed for 150 servings and adjust the proportions accordingly.

Ingredients List for 50 Servings

- 5 kilograms of pasta
- 2 liters of sauce
- 3 kilograms of chicken

Task

1. Calculate the quantities of the ingredients needed for 150 servings.
2. Create a proportional model on paper or digitally that illustrates how the ingredient amounts change with the number of servings.
3. Discuss how the concept of proportion is used in everyday life, providing at least two other examples.

The corresponding proficiency scale for this example is as follows.

1. **Emerging**
   - Calculates the correct quantity of at least one ingredient
   - Attempts to create a model but may have inaccuracies
   - Recognizes proportions in the task but struggles to provide real-life examples

2. **Developing**
   - Correctly calculates the quantities of two of the three ingredients
   - Models the proportional relationships with minor errors
   - Identifies real-life applications of proportions but lacks detailed explanation

3. **Proficient**
   - Accurately calculates the required quantities of all three ingredients
   - Creates a clear and accurate model demonstrating the proportional relationships
   - Explains the concept of proportion using relevant real-life examples, showing good understanding

4. **Advanced**
   - ○ Efficiently calculates the ingredient amounts and explores further implications, such as adjusting for a different number of servings
   - ○ Models the proportions creatively, possibly using digital tools or presenting multiple modeling methods
   - ○ Extends discussion beyond the task, linking proportions to broader mathematical or scientific principles, and suggests innovative real-life applications

This assessment encourages students to deeply engage with mathematical concepts by connecting classroom learning to practical applications. It can be used in various educational contexts.

- **As a project-based learning activity:** Students work in teams to solve the scenario, which encourages collaborative learning and the application of mathematics in team settings.

- **For interactive learning:** During the task, students could use manipulatives or digital tools like spreadsheets to model the proportions, which helps in visualizing and understanding the changes in quantities.

- **As a culminating activity:** To conclude a unit on ratios and proportions, this task assesses students' ability to apply what they've learned in a new and complex situation.

By integrating such assessments into the curriculum, teachers can effectively gauge and enhance students' understanding of key mathematical concepts, fostering deeper engagement and mastery of the subject matter.

Formative Assessment Example: Solving Linear Equations

This formative assessment example particularly supports three key competencies from the CMC framework: (1) conceptual and procedural integration, (2) communication and representation, and (3) logical reasoning and proof. By requiring students to both solve equations and explain their thinking, this assessment evaluates procedural fluency alongside conceptual understanding of algebraic relationships. The progressive complexity of the equations allows students to demonstrate their ability to do the following.

- Apply procedural knowledge while showing conceptual understanding of algebraic principles.
- Communicate mathematical thinking through written explanations.
- Use logical reasoning to justify solution steps.
- Identify mathematical patterns and structures across different problems.

Assessment task: Students are given a set of linear equations to solve. Each equation increases slightly in complexity. The task not only assesses their ability to solve the equations but also requires them to justify their steps and discuss the strategies they used.

Sample Equations

1. $x + 4 = 10$
2. $2x - 5 = 9$
3. $3(x - 1) = 9$
4. $(x + 3) \div 2 = 7$

Students must solve each equation, showing all steps, and then write a brief explanation of the method they used for each. They should also identify any patterns they notice in their strategies across the different equations.

The corresponding proficiency scale is as follows.

1. **Emerging**
    - Correctly solves basic equations—for example, $x + 4 = 10$
    - Attempts more complex equations but often makes errors in steps or operations
    - Struggles to explain or justify the methods used

The CMC Framework in Your Classroom

2. **Developing**
   - Correctly solves basic and moderately complex equations—for example, $2x - 5 = 9$
   - Explains steps with basic reasoning
   - Begins to consistently identify and apply standard strategies

3. **Proficient**
   - Correctly solves all given types of equations, including those with multiple steps—for example, $3(x - 1) = 9$
   - Clearly explains and justifies all steps in the process
   - Identifies patterns and strategies across different problems and explains their effectiveness

4. **Advanced**
   - Solves all equations quickly and accurately, including those with increased complexity—for example, $(x + 3) \div 2 = 7$
   - Articulates a deep understanding of the underlying algebraic principles
   - Suggests multiple methods for solving equations and critiques the efficiency of each method
   - Extends thinking by proposing similar problems with higher complexity or by connecting concepts to real-world scenarios

This assessment and its proficiency scale can be used in various ways.

- **As a diagnostic tool:** Use the assessment at the beginning of a unit to gauge students' prior knowledge and identify focus areas.
- **For ongoing feedback:** As students work through the problems, give them feedback based on the scale to guide their learning and improvement.
- **As a summative assessment:** Use the assessment at the end of the unit to measure student growth and understanding.

In classroom settings, these assessments can be administered individually or in small groups to encourage collaboration and discussion. Additionally, using such structured scales helps teachers provide targeted support and adjust instructional strategies to meet their students' diverse needs, thereby promoting deeper understanding and mastery of mathematical concepts.

Professional Learning

Professional learning is fundamental to successful implementation of the CMC framework, encompassing both individual growth through reflective practice and collective development through collaboration. Research by Powell and colleagues (2020) demonstrates that systematic professional learning significantly impacts teachers' ability to effectively implement new frameworks and improve student outcomes. This finding is reinforced by studies from Doabler and colleagues (2015), showing that teachers who engage in structured professional learning demonstrate greater success in implementing evidence-based mathematics instruction.

Effective professional learning in mathematics education requires the following.

- Systematic reflection on teaching practices
- Regular collaboration with colleagues
- Ongoing assessment of student learning
- Integration of current research and best practices
- Continuous refinement of instructional strategies

The following sections explore two critical components of professional learning: (1) reflective practice and (2) professional development and collaboration. These components work together to create a comprehensive approach to teacher growth and improvement within the CMC framework.

Reflective Practice

Reflective practice involves teachers' deliberate, active contemplation and evaluation of their instructional strategies and classroom dynamics. This reflective process is critical for continual growth and improvement in teaching practices because it ensures that the integration of the CMC framework is effective and also evolves in response to student needs and educational outcomes. The following five strategies support effective reflective practice.

1. **Journaling:** Maintain a reflective journal to document your observations, thoughts, and feelings about daily classroom interactions and the implementation of the CMC framework. This practice allows for structured reflection on what strategies are working, what challenges are emerging, and how students are responding to different instructional approaches.

2. **Student feedback:** Regularly collecting feedback from students about their learning experiences is invaluable. You can do this through anonymous surveys, suggestion boxes, or informal group discussions. Feedback should be specifically directed at understanding students' perspectives on how well the comprehensive mathematical competencies are being integrated into their learning process and how these competencies affect their engagement in and understanding of mathematical concepts.

3. **Peer observations:** Engage in peer observation with colleagues where you visit each other's classrooms to observe, critique, and learn from each other's practice. This peer-review process should focus on the application of the CMC framework and offer constructive feedback on teaching strategies, student interactions, and the classroom environment.

4. **Analysis of student work:** Regularly review student work to identify patterns that might suggest areas of misunderstanding or success. Analyzing how students approach problems, use mathematical language, and apply competencies can provide

deep insights into the effectiveness of instructional strategies and how strategies might be improved.

5. **Video reflection:** Record lessons and review the videos to observe classroom dynamics and instructional delivery from a new perspective. This can help you see things you might miss during the hustle and bustle of a live class, giving you a unique opportunity to critically assess and refine your teaching practices.

You should use the feedback and insights gained from these reflective practices to refine lesson plans, adjust teaching methods, and address student needs more effectively. For instance, if student feedback indicates a lack of understanding of how to apply a specific competency, you might revise the upcoming lessons to include more explicit instruction or practical examples related to that competency. Moreover, this reflective cycle encourages a proactive approach to teaching, where educators continuously seek to enhance their instructional methods to not only meet curricular standards but also better inspire and engage their students. By embedding a culture of reflection, teachers can ensure that their application of the CMC framework is dynamic, responsive, and continually aligned with best educational practices and student learning needs.

Professional Development and Collaboration

Professional development and collaboration are essential aspects of effectively integrating the CMC framework into instructional practices. These elements provide a foundation for teacher growth and community building, crucial for sustained educational success.

Professional learning communities and collaborative teams deliver a structured yet flexible environment for teachers to collaborate, reflect, and grow professionally. Schools and districts should actively facilitate the collaborative process by providing the necessary resources and administrative support, such as allocating time during school hours for collaborative team meetings, offering training on effective collaboration techniques, and creating spaces conducive to group discussions and activities.

Each collaborative team should have a clear focus on one or more competencies of the CMC framework so that teachers can delve deeper into specific competencies and develop specialized knowledge and strategies. For example, one team might concentrate on enhancing problem solving and modeling while another could focus on strategic use of tools and precision. Regular meetings should be scheduled to address ongoing classroom challenges and share timely insights by reviewing recent lessons, planning curriculum integration, and discussing student work or assessment data. To enhance the scope and impact of collaborative teams, schools can establish networks that extend beyond individual districts, enabling access to a broader range of perspectives and resources. Online platforms can facilitate communication and resource sharing among individuals across different locations by hosting virtual meetings, sharing teaching resources, and maintaining ongoing discussions that support the CMC framework's integration into classrooms.

Experienced teachers within collaborative teams can take on mentorship roles, guiding less experienced colleagues through the complexities of integrating the comprehensive mathematical competencies into diverse educational settings. This mentorship can be particularly beneficial for new teachers who are still familiarizing themselves with the CMC framework. Beyond individual growth, collaborative teams can significantly impact the broader educational community by developing and disseminating best practices in teaching mathematics. The collective expertise developed within these communities can lead to more effective instructional strategies that benefit a wider array of students, and can create a dynamic and supportive environment where teachers are empowered to share, learn, and innovate together.

What follows are four additional collaborative strategies that should be part of your professional development framework.

1. **Cross-district workshops and seminars:** Organizing workshops and seminars that bring together teachers from different districts can help disseminate successful teaching

strategies and foster a sense of community among educators. These events can center on specific competencies within the CMC framework and offer hands-on sessions where teachers can experience and learn from varied instructional approaches.

2. **Collaborative planning sessions:** Schools should facilitate regular collaborative planning sessions where teachers can come together to design lessons and units that integrate the comprehensive mathematical competencies. These sessions can help teachers align their curriculum maps and teaching strategies to ensure consistency and coherence in how competencies are taught across different classrooms and grade levels.

3. **Targeted training programs:** Continuous professional development programs focused on the latest educational research and effective practices for integrating the CMC framework should be made available to teachers. These programs might include workshops on innovative teaching methods, conferences featuring leading voices in mathematics education, and specialized courses on advanced pedagogical techniques.

4. **Support from instructional coaches and resources:** Support from instructional coaches is crucial to effectively integrating any new framework into classrooms. Districts should consider employing instructional coaches who specialize in mathematics education to give teachers targeted support. These coaches can directly engage in classroom settings, offering real-time observations and feedback. Their role extends beyond mere observation; they can collaborate with teachers to design lessons, troubleshoot pedagogical challenges, and refine teaching practices that align with the CMC framework. Instructional coaches should also facilitate personalized professional development by identifying specific areas where a teacher can improve or innovate. This might involve demonstrating advanced

problem-solving techniques, introducing digital tools for enhancing student engagement, or providing guidance on how to foster a deeper understanding of mathematical concepts among students. These coaches' support is integral not only in enhancing teachers' instructional strategies but also in building their confidence and proficiency in applying the CMC framework.

In addition to hands-on coaching, it is equally important to provide teachers with access to a comprehensive repository of educational resources. This repository should include a wide array of materials such as peer-reviewed research articles that discuss the latest findings in mathematics education, detailed case studies of successful classroom implementations, instructional video tutorials, and interactive online courses focused on the comprehensive mathematical competencies. These resources will serve as valuable assets for teachers seeking to deepen their knowledge and skills; they offer teachers a variety of approaches and techniques to effectively engage their students.

By combining the personalized support of instructional coaches with access to a rich bank of resources, teachers can continuously evolve their practices to meet the demands of modern classrooms while staying aligned with the CMC framework. This dual approach ensures that teachers receive the necessary support to implement changes and also the necessary tools to innovate and improve their teaching methods over time.

By promoting robust collaboration and offering continuous professional development, schools can ensure that teachers have the skills and knowledge to implement the CMC framework and the support and motivation to do so. These strategies help create a culture of continuous improvement and collective responsibility, which is essential for fostering an educational environment where both students and teachers thrive.

Conclusion

This chapter has explored how to effectively implement the CMC framework through five critical elements: (1) curriculum, (2) planning, (3) instruction, (4) assessment, and (5) professional learning. Through curriculum alignment and thoughtful planning, teachers can systematically integrate the framework's competencies into their daily practice. Strategic instruction ensures these competencies are developed through engaging, student-centered learning experiences. Carefully designed assessments help monitor and guide student growth across all competencies. Finally, ongoing professional learning through reflection and collaboration supports teachers in continuously refining their practice.

The strategies and resources presented here provide a comprehensive tool kit for transforming mathematics education. By implementing these approaches, teachers and students will realize the following benefits.

- Students develop deeper mathematical understanding through integrated competencies.
- Teachers gain confidence in delivering framework-aligned instruction.
- Classrooms become dynamic spaces for mathematical exploration and growth.
- Assessment practices provide meaningful feedback for improvement.
- Professional learning supports continuous educational enhancement.

In your classroom and with your colleagues, take advantage of these strategies and resources to empower students, nurturing mathematical thinkers and well-rounded individuals who are confident in their abilities and ready for all that the future holds. Through systematic implementation of the CMC framework, we can create learning environments where every student has the opportunity to develop comprehensive mathematical proficiency.

EPILOGUE

As we conclude our journey through the CMC framework, we must reflect on the broader landscape of mathematics education. This book has woven together varied observations, conclusions, and recommendations aimed at fostering a more coherent and balanced approach to teaching mathematics. Historically, education reforms have seen various visions for improving curriculum, instruction, and assessment. Yet, too often, initiatives are launched and then prematurely discarded before their efficacy can be fully evaluated. Lessons that could guide future efforts are lost in the shuffle, and strands or elements of mathematical proficiency, particularly those like productive disposition, receive insufficient attention.

The vision presented here is a strategic blueprint designed to ensure that every student develops mathematical proficiency as a cohesive whole. This requires a departure from traditional, piecemeal education policies toward a coordinated and systematic overhaul of how mathematics is taught and learned. Leadership and innovation must drive policy decisions at all levels of the education system to support this profound transformation.

Mathematics is transcending the needs of previous generations; it is no longer confined to a select few. Every student needs to develop a deep understanding of mathematics and its applications to solve problems, reason logically, and make sense of the world. Achieving this means that students must develop all competencies of the CMC framework—conceptual and procedural integration, problem solving and modeling, logical reasoning and proof, communication and representation, strategic use of tools and precision, structural insight and regularity, and productive disposition and engagement—in an integrated fashion.

No nation, not even those leading in international mathematics achievement surveys, has fully achieved mathematical proficiency for all its students. It is an ambitious goal, and no country or governing body will reach it by merely tinkering with individual components of educational policy. Rather, what is needed is a unified approach that reimagines and supports the teaching and learning of mathematics at every level.

In your role as an educator, you are called to be a pioneer in this transformative process. The CMC framework offers a practical pathway to enhancing mathematics education for all students. Through its implementation, you have the opportunity to create a learning environment where the following takes place.

- Students develop deep conceptual understanding alongside procedural fluency.
- Problem solving and modeling connect mathematics to real-world applications.
- Logical reasoning and proof build systematic thinking skills.
- Communication and representation enhance mathematical discourse.
- Strategic tool use and precision support mathematical exploration.
- Structural insight reveals the elegant patterns within mathematics.
- Productive disposition fosters lasting engagement with mathematical thinking.

By adopting this framework, you are not just teaching mathematics; you are preparing a generation to think creatively, solve problems effectively, and approach challenges with confidence and curiosity. Let this book serve not just as a resource but as a catalyst for change, inviting all involved in mathematics education to commit to this comprehensive, thoughtful, and profoundly impactful approach. Together, let's cultivate a future where every student understands mathematics and embraces it as a vital tool for personal and societal advancement.

REFERENCES AND RESOURCES

Ainsworth, S. (2006). DeFT: A conceptual framework for considering learning with multiple representations. *Learning and Instruction, 16*(3), 183–198.

Baroody, A. J. (2003). The development of adaptive expertise and flexibility: The integration of conceptual and procedural knowledge. In A. J. Baroody & A. Dowker (Eds.), *The development of arithmetic concepts and skills: Constructing adaptive expertise* (pp. 1–33). Routledge.

Baroody, A. J., & Ginsburg, H. P. (1986). The relationship between initial meaningful and mechanical knowledge of arithmetic. In J. Hiebert (Ed.), *Conceptual and procedural knowledge: The case of mathematics* (pp. 75–112). Routledge.

Barrett, C. A., & VanDerHeyden, A. M. (2020). A cost-effectiveness analysis of classwide math intervention. *Journal of School Psychology, 80*(1), 54–65. https://doi.org/10.1016/j.jsp.2020.04.002

Boaler, J. (2016). *Mathematical mindsets: Unleashing students' potential through creative math, inspiring messages and innovative teaching.* Jossey-Bass.

Boaler, J. (2022). *Mathematical mindsets: Unleashing students' potential through creative mathematics, inspiring messages and innovative teaching* (2nd ed.). Jossey-Bass.

Borko, H., & Putnam, R. T. (1996). Learning to teach. In D. C. Berliner & R. C. Calfee (Eds.), *Handbook of educational psychology* (pp. 673–708). Macmillan Library Reference USA.

Boston, M. (2012). Assessing instructional quality in mathematics. *Elementary School Journal, 113*(1), 76–104.

Carlson, S. M. (2005). Developmentally sensitive measures of executive function in preschool children. *Developmental Neuropsychology, 28*(2), 595–616. https://doi.org/10.1207/s15326942dn2802_3

Clements, D. H., & Sarama, J. (2021). *Learning and teaching early math: The learning trajectories approach* (3rd ed.). Routledge.

Codding, R. S., Volpe, R. J., & Poncy, B. C. (2017). *Effective math interventions: A guide to improving whole-number knowledge.* Guilford Press.

Cook, S. C., Collins, L. W., Morin, L. L., & Riccomini, P. J. (2020). Schema-based instruction for mathematical word problem solving: An evidence-based review for students with learning disabilities. *Learning Disability Quarterly, 43*(2), 75–87.

Desimone, L. M., & Garet, M. S. (2015). Best practices in teachers' professional development in the United States. *Psychology, Society, and Education, 7*(3), 252–263.

Doabler, C. T., Baker, S. K., Kosty, D. B., Smolkowski, K., Clarke, B., Miller, S. J., et al. (2015). Examining the association between explicit mathematics instruction and student mathematics achievement. *Elementary School Journal, 115*(3), 303–333.

Drijvers, P., Goddijn, A., & Kindt, M. (2011). Algebra education: Exploring topics and themes. In P. Drijvers (Ed.), *Secondary algebra education: Revisiting topics and themes and exploring the unknown* (pp. 5–26). Sense.

Dweck, C. S. (2016). *Mindset: The new psychology of success* (Updated ed.). Random House.

Fey, J. T., & Phillips, E. D. (2009). A course called Algebra I. In C. M. Grant, V. L. Mills, M. Bouck, & E. Davidson (Eds.), *Secondary lenses on learning participant book: Team leadership for mathematics in middle and high schools* (pp. 25–33). Corwin Press.

Fredricks, J. A., Blumenfeld, P. C., & Paris, A. H. (2004). School engagement: Potential of the concept, state of the evidence. *Review of Educational Research, 74*(1), 59–109.

Fuchs, L. S., Newman-Gonchar, R., Schumacher, R., Dougherty, B., Bucka, N., Karp, K. S., et al. (2021). *Assisting students struggling with mathematics: Intervention in the elementary grades* (WWC 2021006). National Center for Education Evaluation and Regional Assistance, Institute of Education Sciences, U.S. Department of Education.

Fuchs, L. S., Wang, A. Y., Preacher, K. J., Malone, A. S., Fuchs, D., & Pachmayr, R. (2021). Addressing challenging mathematics standards with at-risk learners: A randomized controlled trial on the effects of fractions intervention at third grade. *Exceptional Children, 87*(2), 163–182.

Fyfe, E. R., Matthews, P. G., Amsel, E., McEldoon, K. L., & McNeil, N. M. (2018). Assessing formal knowledge of math equivalence among algebra and pre-algebra students. *Journal of Educational Psychology, 110*(1), 87–101.

Hart, S. A., & Ganley, C. M. (2019). The nature of math anxiety in adults: Prevalence and correlates. *Journal of Numerical Cognition, 5*(2), 122–139.

Hattie, J., & Timperley, H. (2007). The power of feedback. *Review of Educational Research, 77*(1), 81–112.

Heijltjes, A., van Gog, T., & Paas, F. (2014). Improving students' critical thinking: Empirical support for explicit instructions combined with practice. *Applied Cognitive Psychology, 28*(4), 518–530.

Hughes, C. A., Morris, J. R., Therrien, W. J., & Benson, S. K. (2017). Explicit instruction: Historical and contemporary contexts. *Learning Disabilities Research and Practice, 32*(3), 140–148.

References and Resources

Hurrell, D. P. (2021). Conceptual knowledge OR procedural knowledge OR conceptual knowledge AND procedural knowledge: Why the conjunction is important for teachers. *Australian Journal of Teacher Education, 46*(2), 57–71. http://dx.doi.org/10.14221/ajte.2021v46n2.4

Hwang, J., & Riccomini, P. J. (2016). Enhancing mathematical problem solving for secondary students with or at risk of learning disabilities: A literature review. *Learning Disabilities Research and Practice, 31*(3), 169–181.

Jacob, R., & Parkinson, J. (2015). The potential for school-based interventions that target executive function to improve academic achievement: A review. *Review of Educational Research, 85*(4), 512–552. https://doi.org/10.3102/0034654314561338

Jitendra, A. K., Nelson, G., Pulles, S. M., Kiss, A. J., & Houseworth, J. (2016). Is mathematical representation of problems an evidence-based strategy for students with mathematics difficulties? *Exceptional Children, 83*(1), 8–25. https://doi.org/10.1177/0014402915625062

Johnston-Wilder, S., & Mason, J. (Eds.). (2005). *Developing thinking in geometry.* Open University.

Kaput, J. J. (1998). Representations, inscriptions, descriptions and learning: A kaleidoscope of windows. *Journal of Mathematical Behavior, 17*(2), 265–281.

Kong, J. E., Yan, C., Serceki, A., & Swanson, H. L. (2021). Word-problem-solving interventions for elementary students with learning disabilities: A selective meta-analysis of the literature. *Learning Disability Quarterly, 44*(4), 248–260.

Kroesbergen, E. H., Van Luit, J. E. H., & Maas, C. J. M. (2004). Effectiveness of explicit and constructivist mathematics instruction for low-achieving students in the Netherlands. *Elementary School Journal, 104*(3), 233–251.

Li, Y., & Bates, T. C. (2020). Testing the association of growth mindset and grades across a challenging transition: Is growth mindset associated with grades? *Intelligence, 81*, Article 101471. https://doi.org/10.1016/j.intell.2020.101471

Loucks-Horsley, S., Stiles, K. E., Mundry, S., Love, N., & Hewson, P. W. (2010). *Designing professional development for teachers of science and mathematics* (3rd ed.). Corwin Press.

Meyer, D. (2011, May 11). *The three acts of a mathematical story* [Blog post]. Accessed at https://blog.mrmeyer.com/2011/the-three-acts-of-a-mathematical-story on November 26, 2024.

Montague, M. (2007). Self-regulation and mathematics instruction. *Learning Disabilities Research and Practice, 22*(1), 75–83.

Moreno, R., & Mayer, R. E. (1999). Cognitive principles of multimedia learning: The role of modality and contiguity. *Journal of Educational Psychology, 91*(2), 358–368.

Morgan, P. L., Farkas, G., & Maczuga, S. (2015). Which instructional practices most help first-grade students with and without mathematics difficulties? *Educational Evaluation and Policy Analysis, 37*(2), 184–205.

Murphy, S., & Ingram, M. (2023). A scoping review of research into mathematics classroom practices and affect. *Teaching and Teacher Education, 132*(1), Article 104235. https://doi.org/10.1016/j.tate.2023.104235

Namkung, J. M., Peng, P., & Lin, X. (2019). The relation between mathematics anxiety and mathematics performance among school-aged students: A meta-analysis. *Review of Educational Research, 89*(3), 459–496.

National Council of Teachers of Mathematics. (2000). *Principles and standards for school mathematics.* Author.

National Council of Teachers of Mathematics. (2014). *Principles to actions: Ensuring mathematical success for all.* Author.

National Governors Association Center for Best Practices & Council of Chief State School Officers. (2010). *Common Core State Standards for mathematics.* Authors. Accessed at https://corestandards.org/wp-content/uploads/2023/09/Math_Standards1.pdf on September 12, 2024.

National Mathematics Advisory Panel. (2008, March). *Foundations for success: The final report of the National Mathematics Advisory Panel.* U.S. Department of Education.

National Research Council. (2001). *Adding it up: Helping children learn mathematics* (J. Kilpatrick, J. Swafford, & B. Findell, Eds.). National Academies Press. Accessed at https://nap.nationalacademies.org/catalog/9822/adding-it-up-helping-children-learn-mathematics on July 29, 2024.

National Research Council. (2005). *How students learn: Mathematics in the classroom.* National Academies Press.

Nation's Report Card. (n.d.a). *NAEP report card: 2022 NAEP mathematics assessment—Highlighted results at grades 4 and 8 for the nation, states, and districts.* Accessed at www.nationsreportcard.gov/highlights/mathematics/2022 on November 13, 2024.

Nation's Report Card. (n.d.b). *NAEP report card: Mathematics.* Accessed at www.nationsreportcard.gov/reports/mathematics/2024/g4_8 on February 13, 2025.

Nelson, G., & McMaster, K. L. (2019). The effects of early numeracy interventions for students in preschool and early elementary: A meta-analysis. *Journal of Educational Psychology, 111*(6), 1001–1022. https://doi.org/10.1037/edu0000334

Opfer, V. D., & Pedder, D. (2011). Conceptualizing teacher professional learning. *Review of Educational Research, 81*(3), 376–407.

Park, D., Gunderson, E. A., Tsukayama, E., Levine, S. C., & Beilock, S. L. (2016). Young children's motivational frameworks and math achievement: Relation to teacher-reported instructional practices, but not teacher theory of intelligence. *Journal of Educational Psychology, 108*(3), 300–313. https://doi.org/10.1037/edu0000064

Passolunghi, M. C., Cargnelutti, E., & Pellizzoni, S. (2019). The relation between cognitive and emotional factors and arithmetic problem-solving. *Educational Studies in Mathematics, 100*(3), 271–290.

Peltier, C., & Vannest, K. J. (2017). A meta-analysis of schema instruction on the problem-solving performance of elementary school students. *Review of Educational Research, 87*(5), 899–920.

Powell, S. R., Doabler, C. T., Akinola, O. A., Therrien, W. J., Maddox, S. A., & Hess, K. E. (2020). A synthesis of elementary mathematics interventions: Comparisons of students with mathematics difficulty with and without comorbid reading difficulty. *Journal of Learning Disabilities, 53*(4), 244–276.

Rittle-Johnson, B. (2017). Developing mathematics knowledge. *Child Development Perspectives, 11*(3), 184–190.

Rittle-Johnson, B., Loehr, A. M., & Durkin, K. (2017). Promoting self-explanation to improve mathematics learning: A meta-analysis and instructional design principles. *ZDM: Mathematics Education, 49*(4), 599–611. http://dx.doi.org/10.1007/s11858-017-0834-z

Rittle-Johnson, B., & Schneider, M. (2015). Developing conceptual and procedural knowledge of mathematics. In R. C. Kadosh & A. Dowker (Eds.), *The Oxford handbook of numerical cognition* (pp. 1118–1134). Oxford University Press. https://doi.org/10.1093/oxfordhb/9780199642342.013.014

Rittle-Johnson, B., Schneider, M., & Star, J. R. (2015). Not a one-way street: Bidirectional relations between procedural and conceptual knowledge of mathematics. *Educational Psychology Review, 27*(4), 587–597.

Schneider, M., Rittle-Johnson, B., & Star, J. R. (2011). Relations among conceptual knowledge, procedural knowledge, and procedural flexibility in two samples differing in prior knowledge. *Developmental Psychology, 47*(6), 1525–1538.

Schneider, M., & Stern, E. (2010). The developmental relations between conceptual and procedural knowledge: A multimethod approach. *Developmental Psychology, 46*(1), 178–192. https://doi.org/10.1037/a0016701

Schneider, W., & Artelt, C. (2010). Metacognition and mathematics education. *ZDM: Mathematics Education, 42*(2), 149–161. https://doi.org/10.1007/s11858-010-0240-2

Schoenfeld, A. H. (1985). Making sense of "out loud" problem-solving protocols. *Journal of Mathematical Behavior, 4*(2), 171–191.

Sfard, A. (2001). There is more to discourse than meets the ears: Looking at thinking as communicating to learn more about mathematical learning. *Educational Studies in Mathematics, 46*(1), 13–57.

Skemp, R. R. (1978). Relational understanding and instrumental understanding. *Arithmetic Teacher, 26*(3), 9–15.

Skinner, E. A., & Pitzer, J. R. (2012). Developmental dynamics of student engagement, coping, and everyday resilience. In S. L. Christenson, A. L. Reschly, & C. Wylie (Eds.), *Handbook of research on student engagement* (pp. 21–44). Springer.

Star, J. R. (2005). Reconceptualizing procedural knowledge. *Journal for Research in Mathematics Education, 36*(5), 404–411.

Stevens, E. A., Rodgers, M. A., & Powell, S. R. (2018). Mathematics interventions for upper elementary and secondary students: A meta-analysis of research. *Remedial and Special Education*, *39*(6), 327–340.

Stockard, J., Wood, T. W., Coughlin, C., & Rasplica Khoury, C. (2018). The effectiveness of direct instruction curricula: A meta-analysis of a half century of research. *Review of Educational Research*, *88*(4), 479–507.

Sweller, J. (2011). Cognitive load theory. In J. P. Mestre & B. H. Ross (Eds.), *The psychology of learning and motivation: Cognition in education* (Vol. 55, pp. 37–76). Elsevier Academic Press.

VanDerHeyden, A. M., & Codding, R. (2020). Belief-based versus evidence-based math assessment and instruction: What school psychologists need to know to improve student outcomes. *Communique*, *48*(5), 1, 20–25.

Vygotsky, L. S. (1978). *Mind in society: The development of higher psychological processes.* Harvard University Press.

Webb, N. M. (2009). The teacher's role in promoting collaborative dialogue in the classroom. *British Journal of Educational Psychology*, *79*(1), 1–28.

Wessman-Enzinger, N. M., & Gerstenschlager, N. E. (2025). *Celebrating mathematical mistakes: How to use students' thinking to unlock understanding.* Solution Tree Press.

Yeager, D. S., & Dweck, C. S. (2012). Mindsets that promote resilience: When students believe that personal characteristics can be developed. *Educational Psychologist*, *47*(4), 302–314.

Yeager, D. S., Hanselman, P., Walton, G. M., Murray, J. S., Crosnoe, R., Muller, C., et al. (2019). A national experiment reveals where a growth mindset improves achievement. *Nature*, *573*(7774), 364–369. https://doi.org/10.1038/s41586-019-1466-y

INDEX

A

abstract representations, 98, 103, 109
  three-act math tasks, 173
active learning strategies
  Charrette protocol, 172–173
  enhance student engagement, 171
  jigsaw method, 174–175
  mathematical tasks, 176-177
  small-group learning, 175–176
  three-act math tasks, 173–174
active participation, 81, 106
adaptability, 92, 104
adapting questions, 194
adaptive reasoning, 5
Adding It Up (National Research Council), 5
Addition, 59–60, 63
  applying algorithms to new contexts, 156
  conceptual and procedural integration, 188
  encouraging generalization, 152
  highlighting patterns and structures, 150
  integration in teaching, 43
  mathematical tasks, 177
  real-world applications, 78
  reflective discussion on mathematical
    structures, 157
  story problems, 112
Ainsworth, S., 100
algebra, 41–44
  algorithm variations, 154–155
  encouraging generalization, 153
  financial literacy, 63–64
  introducing algorithms as conceptual
    tools, 149
  paradigm shift in teaching, 121
  pattern recognition, 144
algebra tiles, 132
algebraic application, 62
algebraic concepts, 105

algebraic equations, 64, 64, 75–76
algebraic expressions, 42, 44
algebraic functions, 191
algebraic manipulations, 121
algebraic method, 54
algebraic modeling, 48, 57
algebraic operations, 124
algebraic software, 44
algebraic symbols, 99
algorithms, 41–42, 143
  applying to a new context, 155–157
  as conceptual tools, 148–150
  Euclidean, 151
  exploring variations, 153–155
all means all, 13, 219
Amsel, E., 37
analysis of student work, 213–214
analytical discussion, 84–86
  example, 84–85
angle-side-angle condition, 80
applying algorithms to new context, 155–157
  examples, 155–156
arithmetic skills, 52
  pattern recognition, 144
  small-group learning, 176
Artelt, C., 180
articulation of reasoning, 95
assessment, 110, 130, 187
  CMC framework, 206
  digital tools, 130
  formative assessment examples, 207–212
automaticity, 19–20
  defined, 19

B

bar models, 125
Barrett, C. A., 163
base-ten blocks, 97, 100, 103, 132, 141, 150
  virtual, 127

base-ten operations, 189
Bates, T. C., 12, 21, 83, 163
bead-sliding tools, 127
beginning-of-class routines, 200, 203
Beilock, S. L., 12
Benson, S. K., 80
blended learning, 131
blocks, 43, 99, 105
    base-ten, 97, 100, 103, 127, 132, 141, 150
    logic, 132
Boaler, J., 116
break-even analysis, 55
budgeting, 62–63, 172
building mathematical communication, 106–107

C

calculating area, 60–61
calculating costs, profits, and losses, 177
calculators, 32–33, 62, 123
    graphing, 121, 124, 141, 44
    scientific, 124, 135
calculus
    Charrette protocol, 173
    concepts, 105
    problem solving and monitoring, 191
    problems, 113, 116
    strategic use of tools and precision, 191
Cargnelutti, E., 83
Carlson, S. M., 74
Celebrating Mathematical Mistakes (Wessman-Enzinger & Gertenschlager), 183
characterizing mathematics as more than memorization, 15–17
Charrette protocol, 172–173, 185
charts, 106
ChatGPT, 130
chips, 132
choosing appropriate representations, 109
choosing appropriate solution methods, 111
circle apps, 125
CK–12 Foundation, 129
class debates, 91, 115
class discussions, 119
    encouraging, 205
    on mathematical structures, 157–158
    reflection and, 67, 88
class discussions, 178
classroom interaction, 204–205
Clements, D. H., 50
closure routines, 200, 204
Codding, R. S., 14, 22, 123, 162–164, 168, 168
cognitive load theory (Sweller), 114

collaboration, 214
    cross-district workshops and seminars, 215–216
    instructional coaches and resources, 216–217
    planning sessions, 216
    professional learning, 214–217
    targeted training programs, 216
collaborative problem solving, 65–66
    analytical discussion, 86example, 65
    projects, 106
Collins, L. W., 47
Common Core State Standards, 4–5
communication and representation skills, 2–3, 7, 81, 95–97, 120, 178, 183
    analytical discussion, 86
    building mathematical communication, 106–107
    CFC framework and, 5
    content and goals, 197
    criteria for effective representations, 103–104
    essence of, 96–111
    implementing criteria, 105–107
    justification skills, 108–110
    multiple methods of expression, 108
    progressive development of representations, 97–103
    progressive vocabulary development, 107–108
    scope-and-sequence implementation, 189, 191
    strategies to enhance, 111–120
compartmentalization, 33–35
competency integration, 33–35
    task example, 35
complex functions, 158
complex numbers, 154
comprehensive mathematical competency (CMC) framework, 2–6
    assessment, 187, 206–212
    curriculum, 187–195
    image, 3
    in your classroom, 187–188, 218
    instruction, 187, 199–205
    planning, 187, 196–199
    professional learning, 187, 212–217
computers, 32
conceptual and procedural integration, 2–3, 6, 10–11, 15–16, 26, 45–46
    content and goals, 196–197
    essence of, 25–38
    examples, 26–27, 40–42
    scope-and-sequence implementation, 188–190
    strategies to enhance, 38–45
conceptual understanding, 5, 26–28, 220
    defined, 25–26

importance of multiple representations, 28–29

interplay with logical reasoning, 76–77

interplay with problem solving, modeling, and procedural fluency, 58–60

role of knowledge clusters, 30–31

strategies to enhance, 40–41

vs. memorizing, 26–27

conducting action research, 195

confidence, 83

fostering, 11

mathematical discussions, 183–184

representational fluidity, 114

congruency, 79–80

similarity and, 191

constructing logical arguments, 89–92, 175

example, 90–91

constructive challenge, 21–22

constructive criticism, 117, 178

content and goals, 196–198

continuity and integration, 198

converting between verbal and mathematical symbols, 109

Cook, S. C., 47, 144, 153, 156

Coughlin, C., 14

counters, 99, 105

COVID-19 pandemic, 2–3

creating a repository, 194

creating a supportive learning environment, 169–170

examples, 169–170

creating environments that balance skill development and conceptual understanding, 11

criteria for effective representations, 103

adaptability, 104

precision, 104

streamlining, 104

visibility, 103

critical listening and peer review, 115–117

examples, 115–116

mathematical writing, 138–139

peer-review sessions, 116

critical thinking

analytical discussion, 85

encouraging, 178–180

error analysis, 81–83

journaling, 171

mathematical tasks, 176

representations, 99–100

Socratic dialogue, 81

cross-district workshops and seminars, 215–216

Cuisenaire rods, 132, 141

culminating activities, 209

cultivating inventive problem-solving skills, 53

developing effective modeling techniques, 56–58

flexible thinking, 55–56

interplay of problem solving, modeling, procedural fluency, and conceptual understanding, 58–60

mathematical problem types, 53–54

cumulative learning experiences, 20

curiosity, 169

curriculum, 187-188

alignment, 193–196

modify and elevate questions, 194

plan for implementation, 195

prioritize continuous feedback, 195

review and select suitable problems, 193–194

scope-and-sequence implementation, 188–193

D

data handling and analysis, 65, 124

pattern recognition, 144–145

small-group learning, 176

data-based decision making, 14

decimals

mathematical tasks, 177

problem solving and modeling, 189

real-world applications, 78

strategic use of tools and precision, 189

decision making, 72

declining proficiency in mathematics skills, 2–3

decomposition, 60–61

deeper understanding, 81

through representation, 119

designing follow-up questions, 194

Desimone, L. M., 165–166

desirable difficulty, 22

Desmos, 128, 134–135

developing effective modeling techniques, 56–58

development and application of logical reasoning and proof, 74–76

at an early age, 74

development of communication and representation skills. *See* communication and representation skills

diagrams, 95, 100, 105

differential equations, 49

differentiated learning, 175

digital portfolios, 170

digital tools, 112, 125–131, 191

direct, 130

digital vocabulary cards, 126

direct application of formulas, 61

distinct but interwoven competency, 147–148

diverse learning styles, 100

diverse proof techniques, 86–89
  example, 87
diverse representations, 7
division, 74–75
Doabler, C. T., 121–122, 133, 168, 212
documenting, 195
Drijvers, P., 121–122
during-class routines, 200-201, 203–204
Durkin, K., 180
Dweck, C. S., 12
dynamic software, 121, 141

E

educational equity and accessibility, 13
encouraging constructive challenge, 21–22
encouraging generalization, 152–153
  examples, 152–153
encouraging reflective and critical thinking, 178–180
  examples, 178–179
engagement (*see also* productive disposition and
  engagement), 162–163, 166–167
    analytical discussion, 86
    construction of logical arguments, 92
enhanced analytical skills, 91
enhanced communication through discussion, 119
enhanced learning through simulation, 124–125
enhanced listening skills, 116
enhanced logical thinking, 88–89
enhanced understanding, 85
enhancing engagement through active listening
  strategies, 171
    Charette protocol, 172–173
    jigsaw method, 174–175
    mathematical tasks, 176–178
    small-group learning, 175–176
    three-act math tasks, 173–174
error analysis, 81–84
  example, 82
essence of communication and representation, 96–97
    development of communication and
      representation skills, 97–110
    interplay of communications
      and representations and other
      competencies, 110–111
essence of conceptual and procedural
  integration, 25–26
    competency integration, 33–35
    conceptual understanding, 26–31
    power of integrated mathematics
      learning, 35–38
    procedural fluency, 31–33
essence of logical reasoning and proof, 72–74
  development and application of, 74–76

interplay between logical reasoning and
  other competencies, 76–79
essence of problem solving and modeling, 49–53
    cultivating inventive problem-solving
      skills, 53–60
essence of productive disposition and
  engagement, 162–163
    engagement, 166–167
    interplay across competencies, 168–169
    productive disposition through systematic
      instruction, 163–166
    three-act math tasks, 173–174
essence of strategic use of tools and precision,
  123–125
    digital tools, 125–131
    interplay between tool use and other
      competencies, 131–134
essence of structural insight and regularity, 145–145
    importance of, 146
    distinct yet interwoven competency, 147–148
estimating, 64
    collaborative problem solving, 65
    examples, 40–44
    mathematical problem types, 54
    real-world applications, 77
    reflection in problem solving, 67
    using known measurements, 61
Euclidean algorithms, 151
evaluating existing problems, 193
evaluating the effectiveness of different
  approaches, 109
evaluation, 110
examples
    analytical discussion, 84–85
    applying algorithms to new contexts, 155–156
    Charette protocol, 172–173
    collaborative problem solving, 65
    competency integration, 35
    conceptual understanding, 26–27, 40–42
    construction of logical arguments, 89–91
    creating a supportive learning environ,
      169–170
    critical listening and peer review, 115–116
    diverse proof techniques, 87
    encouraging reflective and critical
      thinking, 178–180
    error analysis, 82
    exploration of multiple solutions, 60–61
    exploring algorithm variations, 154–155
    formative assessment, 207–212
    highlighting patterns and structures, 150–151
    integration in teaching, 43–44
    introducing algorithms as conceptual
      tools, 149

Index

jigsaw method, 174–175
lesson design template, 200–202
mathematical problem types, 54
mathematical tasks, 177
modeling a passion for mathematics, 180–181
modeling and fostering meticulous problem–solving techniques, 139–140
precision in problem statements, 136–137
procedural fluency, 41–42
process over product, 67
progressive development of representations, 102
progressive vocabulary development, 107–108
promoting mathematical discussions, 118–119
real-life scenarios, 62–64
reflective discussion on mathematical structures, 157–158
scope-and-sequence implementation, 188–192
Socratic dialogue, 79–80
three-act math tasks, 173–174
varied forms of expression, 112–113
explaining why a strategy works, 109
explicit instruction, 22, 80
digital tools, 135–136
exploring algorithm variations, 153–155
examples, 154–155
exploring multiple solutions, 60–61
examples, 60–61
exponential functions, 177

F

fairness, 91
Farkas, G., 74
feedback, 88, 172
consistent, 137
constructive criticism, 117
digital tools, 130
gathering, 195
immediate, 115
prioritizing, 195
specific, 14
student, 213
financial literacy, 177
fixed vs. growth mindset, 12–13
flexible thinking, 55–56
diverse proof techniques, 89
gaining, 68
in problem solving, 61, 52–53
flipped classroom, 131
fluency
misunderstandings about, 17–21
formative assessment examples, 207–212

fostering a community of mathematical inquiry, 182–184
examples, 182–183
fraction circles, 103
fraction representation tools, 125
fraction strips, 98
fraction tiles, 132, 141
fractions, 40–43, 63
communication and representation, 191
problem solving and modeling, 189
strategic use of tools and precision, 189
Fuchs, L. S., 6, 28, 114, 123, 163
Fyfe, E. R., 37

G

Ganley, C. M., 162, 181
Garet, M. S., 165–166
Gathering student feedback, 195
Generalization, 152–153
GeoGebra, 128, 135
geography, 156
geometric properties, 191
geometric reasoning, 49, 60–61
visual accuracy in, 124
geometric transformations, 112
geometry
encouraging generalization, 152
jigsaw method, 174–175
pattern recognition, 144
Gertenschlager, N. E., 183
goal setting, 170
Godding, A., 122
Google Sheets, 62
graphical representation, 57, 121–122
graphing calculators, 121, 124
graphs, 95, 105–106, 113
group discussions. *See* class discussions
group work, 106
dynamics, 170
grouping, 74
growth mindset, 21–22
error analysis, 83
cultivating, 170–171
vs. fixed, 12–13
guest lecturers, 181
guided dialogue, 80
guided practice, 88
Gunderson, E. A., 12

H

Hart, S. A., 162, 181
Hattie, J., 117

Heijltjes, A., 80, 85, 88–89, 91, 108–109, 111, 158, 171, 177–178

highlighting patterns and structures, 143–144, 146, 150–152
    encouraging generalization, 152–153
    examples, 150–151

Houseworth, J., 114

how the CMC framework addresses myths and misconceptions, 11
    refuting the notion of inherent ability, 12–22

Hughes, C. A., 80, 122, 168

Hwang, J., 86, 96, 101, 107, 110, 119, 132, 181–182

I

identifying and correcting errors, 109

identifying key concepts, 193

implementing criteria in instructional practices, 105–107

implementing effective skill-building instruction, 14

importance of structural insight and regularity, 146

improved communication, 116

indirect proof, 87

individual exploration, 130

informal language, 107

inherent ability myth, 12–15

instruction, 187, 199
    classroom interaction, 204–205
    lesson design, 199–202
    preparation for the lesson, 203–204

instructional coaches and resources, 216–217

integrated learning experiences, 119

integrating instructional approaches, 20, 43–45
    examples, 43–44
    power of, 35–38

integrating technology and tools, 68–70

interactive clock apps, 126

interactive learning, 209

interdisciplinary challenges, 156

intermodal translation, 113

interplay across competencies, 168–169

interplay of communications and representations and other competencies, 110–111

interplay of logical reasoning and other competencies, 76–79

interplay of problem solving, modeling, procedural fluency, and conceptual understanding, 58–60

interplay of tool use and other competencies, 131–134

interpretation and decision making, 48

introducing algorithms as conceptual tools, 148–150
    examples, 149

J

Jacob, R., 74

jigsaw method, 174–175
    examples, 174–175

Jitendra, A. K., 114

Johnston-Wilder, S., 144

journaling, 171, 213

justification skills, 107–109, 111
    assessment considerations, 109–110
    classroom implementation, 109
    communication, 95
    mathematical ideas, 72–74
    translation abilities, 109

K

Kaput, J. J., 114

Khan Academy, 128

Khoury, C. R., 14

Kindt, M., 122

Kiss, A. J., 114

knowledge clusters, 30–31

Kong, J. E., 6, 47, 114

Kroesbergen, E. H., 81

L

leadership skills, 183

learning goals, 14

lesson design, 199–202
    template, 200–202

Levine, S. C., 12

Li, Y., 12, 21, 83, 163

life-long learners, 165–166

Lin, X., 162

linear equations
    assessment example, 209–212
    highlighting patterns and structures, 151

Loehr, A. M., 179–180

logic blocks, 132

logical reasoning and proof, 2–3, 7, 71–72, 92–93, 147, 220
    CFC framework and, 5
    content and goals, 197
    essence of, 72–79
    scope-and-sequence implementation, 189, 191
    strategies to enhance, 78–92

M

Maas, C. J. M., 81

Maczuga, S., 74

manipulatives, 32, 40, 74, 99, 112, 123, 133, 141, 150, 176, 178
    digital, 134

Index

geometric, 132
virtual money, 126
Mason, J., 144
"math congress," 178
math talk circles, 115, 182
math wall, 183
mathematic explanation sessions, 118
mathematical communication
building, 6, 106–107
formal and informal, 109
modeling, 109
multiple modes of expression, 108
progressive vocabulary development, 107–108
mathematical discussions, 109, 138
mathematical language
mathematical discussions, 183–184
mathematical tasks, 177
tools and, 133
mathematical mindsets, 23
mathematical operations, 177
mathematical problem types, 53–54
examples, 54
mathematical tasks, 176–178
examples, 177
mathematical theory forums, 118–119
mathematical thinking, 11
mathematics understanding, 89
Mathway, 129
Matthews, P. G., 37
McEldoon, K. L., 37
McMaster, K. L., 14, 33, 177
McNeil, N. M., 37
measurement tools, 189
memorizing, 10
mathematics is more than, 15–17
vs. conceptual understanding, 26–27
meta-analysis, 177
metacognition, 68
methods of representation, 118
Meyer, D., 173
Microsoft Copilot, 130
Microsoft Excel, 62
Microsoft Math Solver, 129
minimizing misunderstandings about speed and fluency, 17–21
misconceptions. *See* myths and misconceptions
mnemonic devices, 18
modeling a passion for mathematics, 180–182, 186
examples, 180–181
modeling and fostering meticulous problem-solving techniques, 139–140
accurate tool use, 133
examples, 139–140

high-level performance, 167
mathematical communication, 109
precision, 138
modifying and elevating questions, 194
monitoring and strategy adjustment, 77
Montague, M., 86, 92
Morgan, P. L., 68, 74, 91, 96–97, 101, 105–107, 107, 111, 119, 132, 163, 165, 168, 182, 184
Morin, L. L., 47
Morris, J. R., 80
Moston, M., 165
moving between mathematical representations, 109
multiple modes of expression, 107–108
multiple representations, 28–29
multiple solution strategies, 175
multiplication visualization, 127
multiplication
algorithm variations, 154
conceptual and procedural integration, 189
for larger numbers, 75
introducing algorithms as conceptual tools, 149
real-world applications, 77
real-world scenarios, 63, 74–75
reflective discussion on mathematical structures, 157
using base-ten blocks, 16
myths and misconceptions, 7, 9–11, 24
how the CMC framework addresses, 11–22
mathematical discussions, 183–184
role of educators in shaping mindsets, 23

N

Namkung, J. M., 162
National Assessment of Educational Progress, 4
National Council of Teachers of Mathematics, 4–5, 22, 155
National Mathematics Advisory Panel, 4
National Research Council, 5, 162
need for a new framework, 4–6
Nelson, G., 14, 33, 114, 177
Newman-Gonchar, 4, 6, 28, 114, 123, 163
nonroutine problems, 58–59
number charts, 126
number frames, 126
number grabbing, 50
Number Line by Brainingcamp, 129
number lines, 97, 99
apps, 126
digital, 134–135
virtual, 126–127
number operations, 189
number patterns, 152

number pieces, 127
number rack, 127
number-partitioning activities, 74
numerical operations, 191

O

Opfer, V. D., 165
optimization, 49
    models, 57
organizing workshop sessions, 194

P

Paas, F., 80
Park, D., 12, 171
Parkinson, J., 74
partial product finder, 127
Passolunghi, M. C., 83, 162, 181
pattern blocks, 133
    virtual, 127
pattern recognition (*see also* highlighting patterns; patterns), 143–144, 146
    importance of, 144–145
patterns. *See also* highlighting patterns; pattern recognition)
    in number systems and algebraic structures, 191
    structural insight and regularity, 190
pedagogy, 63–64
Pedder, D., 165
peer observations, 213
peer review. *See* critical listening and peer review
peer-led teaching, 175, 183
Pellizzoni, S., 83
Peltier, C., 48
Peng, P., 162
percentages, 63
percentiles, 177
PhET Interactive Simulations, 128–129
physical models, 95, 98–100
planning, 187, 196–199
    content and goals, 196–198
    continuity and integration, 198
    for implementation, 195
    student-centered approach, 198
planning sessions, 216
Poncy, B. C., 14
Powell, S. R., 6, 14, 17, 28–29, 31, 33, 36, 85, 89, 91, 96–97, 100–101, 103, 109–110, 114, 119, 121, 132, 134, 144, 150–153, 155–158, 163–164, 168, 183–184, 212
precise mathematical terms, 108
precision (*see also* strategic use of tools and precision), 104, 133–134

defined, 122
examples, 136–137
in calculations, 124
in problem statements, 136–138
modeling, 138
preparation for the lesson, 200, 203
    beginning-of-class routines, 203
    closure routines, 204
    during-class routines, 203–204
prioritizing continuous feedback, 195
probability, 190–191
problem solving and modeling, 7, 2–3, 47–49, 69–70, 220
    analytical discussion, 84–85
    CFC framework and, 5
    content and goals, 197
    cultivating inventive, 53–60
    diverse proof techniques, 89
    error analysis, 83
    essence of, 49–60
    explanation of, 95
    integrating fluency practice with, 18
    interplay with logical reasoning, 76
    journaling, 171
    logical reasoning and proof, 72
    mathematical discussions, 118, 183–184
    mathematical tasks, 176
    pattern recognition, 145, 147–148
    representations, 99–100
    scope-and-sequence implementation, 189–191
    software tools, 124
    strategies to enhance, 60–68
    three-act math tasks, 173–174
procedural fluency (*see also* conceptual and procedural integration), 5, 10, 31–33, 220
    CFC framework and, 5
    defined, 26
    examples, 41–42
    interplay with logical reasoning, 77
    interplay with problem solving, modeling, and conceptual understanding, 58–60
    strategies to enhance, 41–43
process over product, 66–68
    example, 67
productive disposition and engagement, 2–3, 5, 7, 53–54, 220
    CFC framework and, 5
    content and goals, 198
    essence of, 162–169
    scope-and-sequence implementation, 190, 192
    strategies to enhance, 169–185
professional development, 195, 214–217

Index

professional learning, 187, 212
    professional development and collaboration, 214–217
    reflective practice, 213–214
proficiency scales, 208–211
progression from accuracy to fluency, 18
progressive vocabulary development, 107–108
    examples, 102
project-based learning, 180–181, 209
projectile motion, 174
promoting mathematical discussion, 117–120
    examples, 118–119
proof. *See also* logical reasoning and proof
    by contradiction, 87
properties of multiplication, 30
properties of operations, 189
proportional reasoning, 174, 190
    assessment example, 207–209
    real-world applications, 77
Pulles, S. M., 114

Q

quadratic equations, 113
quadratic functions, 174
questioning, 169
questions
    adapting, 194
    critical, 122
    myths and misconceptions, 24

R

ratio concepts, 40–41, 43–44
    cultural and procedural integration, 190
    strategy, 55
real-world scenarios
    applying algorithms to new contexts, 155–156
    conceptual understanding, 40–41
    construction of logical arguments, 89–92
    examples, 62–64
    flexible thinking, 55–56
    integration in teaching, 43–45
    logical reasoning and proof, 74–75
    mathematical problem types, 54
    mathematical tasks, 177
    mathematical theory forums, 118–119
    modeling, 49
    multiplication, 77
    procedural fluency, 41–43
    project-based learning, 180–181
    reflective and critical thinking, 179
    small-group learning, 176
    Socratic dialogue, 79–80

storytelling, 180
three-act math tasks, 174
translational practice, 113
using, 61–65
recognizing and using patterns, 7
recognizing how misconceptions influence teaching practices and student engagement, 11
reflection, 88
    on reasoning, 91
    video, 214
reflective and adaptive learning, 20
reflective discussions on mathematical structures, 157–158
    examples, 157–158
reflective meetings, 195
reflective practice, 170, 213–214
    encouraging, 178–180
refuting the notion of inherent ability, 12–15
    characterizing mathematics as more than memorization, 15–17
    encouraging constructive challenge, 21–22
    minimizing misunderstandings about speed and fluency, 17–21
reinforcement through practice, 91
relational understanding, 30–31
replacing limiting beliefs with evidence-based approaches, 11
reports, 106
representation. *See* communication and representation
representational fluidity, 114
reproductive thinking, 53
resilience, 68
reviewing and selecting suitable problems, 193–194
Riccomini, P. J., 47, 86, 96, 101, 107, 110, 119, 132, 181–182
Rittle-Johnson, B., 15–17, 28–29, 31, 33, 36, 83, 85, 110, 119, 132, 144, 150, 151, 153, 155, 157–158, 179–180
Rodgers, M. A., 14
role of educators in shaping mindsets, 23
routine problems, 58–59
    vs. nonroutine problems, 53
rubrics, 109

S

Sarama, J., 50
scaffolding, 166–167, 185, 203
schema-based instruction, 47–48
Schneider, M., 15–17, 29, 31, 36–37, 85, 88–89, 92, 110, 143, 150, 153, 155, 157–158, 179, 183, 180
Schoenfeld, A. H., 47

science
  applying algorithms to new contexts, 156
  of mathematics movement, 6
scientific calculators, 124
scope-and-sequence implementation, 188–193
  examples, 188–192
self-explanation, 179
sequence of implementation, 195
Serceki, A., 6
seven essential competencies, 2–3
Sfard, A., 95–96
sharing findings, 194
sharing lesson plans, 195
side-angle-side postulate, 80
simulation models, 57
Skemp, R. R., 31
small-group learning, 175–176, 185
  examples, 175–176
societal issues, 177
Socratic dialogue, 79–81
  examples, 79–81
software, 123–124
  dynamic, 141
soliciting peer review, 194
spatial reasoning, 112
speed, 10, 12
  misunderstandings about, 17–21
spreadsheet software, 62
Star, J. R., 15, 17, 36
statistical analysis, 48, 116
statistical models, 57, 113
statistics, 65
  problem solving and monitoring, 190–191
  small-group learning, 176
  strategic use of tools and precision, 191
Stern, E., 31, 37, 83, 88–89, 151
Stevens, E. A., 14, 123, 182
Stockard, J., 14
story problems, 112
  problem solving and modeling, 189
  using chips, 132
storytelling, 180
strategic competence, 5
strategic thinking, 6
strategic use of tools and precision, 2–3, 7,
  121–123, 141–142, 220
  CFC framework and, 5
  content and goals, 197
  essence of, 123–134
  scope-and-sequence implementation, 189, 191
  strategies to enhance, 134–140
strategies to enhance communication and
  representation, 111–112

critical listening and peer review, 115–117
promoting mathematical discussion, 117–120
varied forms of expression, 112–115
strategies to enhance conceptual and procedural
  integration, 38–40
  conceptual understanding, 40–41
  integration in teaching, 43–45
  procedural fluency, 41–43
strategies to enhance logical reasoning and
  proof, 78–79
  analytical discussion, 84–86
  constructing logical arguments, 89–92
  diverse proof techniques, 86–89
  error analysis, 81–84
  Socratic dialogue, 79–81
strategies to enhance problem solving and
  modeling, 60
  collaborative problem solving, 65–66
  exploring multiple solutions, 60–61
  process over product, 66–68
  real-life scenarios, 61–65
strategies to enhance productive disposition and
  engagement, 169
  creating a supportive learning
    environment, 169–171
  encouraging reflective and critical
    thinking, 178–180
  enhancing engagement through active
    listening strategies, 171–173
  fostering a community of mathematical
    inquiry, 182–185
  modeling a passion for mathematics, 180–182
strategies to enhance strategic use of tools and
  precision, 134–136
  modeling and fostering meticulous
    problem-solving techniques, 139–140
  peer review of mathematical writing, 138–139
  precision in problem statements, 136–138
  symbol usage workshops, 138
strategies to enhance structural insight and
  regularity, 148
  applying algorithms to new contexts, 155–157
  encouraging generalization, 152–153
  exploring algorithm variations, 153–155
  highlighting patterns and structures, 150–152
  introducing algorithms as conceptual
    tools, 148–150
  reflective discussions on mathematical
    structures, 157–158
streamlining, 104
structural insight and regularity, 2–3, 7, 143,
  158–160, 220
  CFC framework and, 5
  content and goals, 197
  essence of, 143–148

importance of, 146
pattern recognition, 145
scope-and-sequence implementation, 190–191
strategies to enhance, 148–158
structured debates, 115
structured protocols, 109
student feedback, 213
gathering, 195
student-centered approach, 198
subtraction, 59–60
applying algorithms to new contexts, 156
conceptual and procedural integration, 188
integration in teaching, 43
mathematical tasks, 177
real-world applications, 78
reflective discussion on mathematical structures, 157
story problems, 112
supporting productive learning behaviors, 14
supporting solutions with logical arguments, 109
Swanson, H. L., 6
Sweller, J., 114
symbolic notation, 99, 103, 105
symbols, 95, 100
usage workshop, 138
symmetry, 127
systematic instruction
productive disposition through, 163–166
systematic trial and error, 54
systems of equations and inequality, 64

T

targeted training programs, 216
technology, 44
graphing, 113
integrating, 68–70
strategic use of, 2–3, 7, 121–142
tessellation, 127
Therrien, W. J., 80
think-pair-share, 200
thought process documentation, 66–67
three-act math tasks, 173–174, 185
examples, 173–174
time management, 167
timed practice, 17–18
Timperley, H., 117
tools as a reward system, 169–170
total cost modeling, 55
traditional approaches, 1
vs. needs of 21st century learners, 4–5
transferable skills, 89
transitional language, 108

translating between concrete and abstract representations, 109
translating verbal description into mathematical representations, 111
translation abilities, 107
translational practice, 113
trigonometric functions, 191
jigsaw method, 175
Tsukayama, E., 12

U

unified approach to mathematics education, 8
Unifix cubes, 133
unit cost calculation, 56
usage and demand modeling, 56

V

van Gog, T., 80
Van Luit, H. E. H., 81
VanDerHeyden, A. M., 123, 162–164, 168
Vannest, K. J., 48
varied forms of expression, 112–115
examples, 112–113
verbal communication, 100, 108–109
translating descriptions into mathematical representations, 111
video reflection, 214
virtual geoboards, 125
virtual money manipulatives, 126
visibility, 103
visual communication, 108
visual representation, 38–39, 54, 63, 95, 100, 113
visualizing, 75, 112
Volpe, R. J., 14
Vygotsky, L. S., 22

W

Wang, A. Y., 36, 163
Webb, N. M., 116–117
Wessman-Enzinger, N. M., 183
WolframAlpha, 129–130
Wood, T. W., 14
word problems. *See* story problems
written communication, 108–109

Y

Yan, C., 6
Yeager et, 171
Yeager, D. S., 12, 21–22

Z

zone of proximal development (Vygotsky), 22

The New Art and Science of Teaching Mathematics
Nathan D. Lang-Raad and Robert J. Marzano
Discover how to make the most of the groundbreaking New Art and Science of Teaching model in mathematics classrooms. Readers will discover myriad strategies and tools for articulating learning goals, conducting lessons, tracking students' progress, and more.
BKF810

Renaissance Thinking in the Classroom
Nathan D. Lang-Raad
In this book, Nathan D. Lang-Raad details nine specific habits of thinking and a challenge-based framework that educators should systematically integrate to promote students' academic knowledge and lifelong learning. Using this guide, teachers can design lessons that foster necessary behaviors.
BKG127

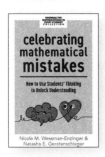

Celebrating Mathematical Mistakes
Nicole M. Wessman-Enzinger and Natasha E. Gerstenschlager
In this practical guide, Wessman-Enzinger and Gerstenschlager provide a foundation for celebrating mathematical mistakes, offering strategies and task structures that encourage creative mathematical reasoning. This book moves beyond the correct–incorrect paradigm by acknowledging the beauty, power, and ubiquity of mistakes.
BKG178

See It, Say It, Symbolize It
Patrick L. Sullivan
Reimagine elementary mathematics pedagogy using a three-step process. By helping students develop a language that is consistent across concepts and connecting it to what is seen and symbolized, teachers empower their students to engage in reasoning they will utilize throughout their lives.
BKG187

Solution Tree | Press

Visit SolutionTree.com or call 800.733.6786 to order.